Francis Peloubet

Select songs No. 2

For the singing service in the prayer meeting, Sunday school, Christian endeavor meetings

Francis Peloubet

Select songs No. 2
For the singing service in the prayer meeting, Sunday school, Christian endeavor meetings

ISBN/EAN: 9783337265106

Printed in Europe, USA, Canada, Australia, Japan

Cover: Foto ©Lupo / pixelio.de

More available books at **www.hansebooks.com**

Select Songs

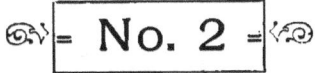

= No. 2 =

FOR THE

SINGING SERVICE

IN THE

Prayer Meeting;

Sunday School;

Christian Endeavor Meetings.

EDITED BY

F. N. PELOUBET, D. D. AND **HUBERT P. MAIN.**

THE BIGLOW & MAIN CO.

76 East Ninth Street,   215 Wabash Avenue,
New York.   Chicago.

May be Ordered of Booksellers and Music Dealers.

COPYRIGHT, 1893, BY THE BIGLOW & MAIN CO.

PREFACE.

SELECT SONGS No. 1 has been received with so great favor, and has so well filled a place otherwise left vacant, that the compilers feel warranted in preparing another work, projected on the same lines and selected from the abundance of excellent material gathered in the course of ordinary duties in practical Sunday School work during the ten years since SELECT SONGS No. 1 was issued.

SELECT SONGS No. 2 contains no pieces that are in No. 1 excepting a few pages of familiar hymns, with a line of melody added for convenience in leading the singing, and which are placed at the end of the book.

There are very great advantages in using as far as possible the same book in the Prayer-meeting, the Sunday School and the Christian Endeavor meeting, instead of having three separate works and three separate sets of hymns and tunes. Thus the gain through the service of song in one department is gained for all.

The choicest words and music that are adapted to the purpose have been selected.

Special thanks are due to the many kind friends who have given their judgment from the standpoints of professor of music, choir leader, pastor, superintendent of Sunday School, and leader of song in the prayer-meeting, and to OLIVER DITSON CO., THE JOHN CHURCH CO., MAYNARD, MERRILL & CO., JOHN J. HOOD, W. J. BALTZELL, U. P. BOARD OF PUBLICATION, Rev. J. E. RANKIN, D.D., WILL. L. THOMPSON, Rev. J. M. DRIVER, Rev. F. M. LAMB, WM. G. FISCHER, and others for permission to use valuable selections of which they own the copyright.

Much of the music and words is copyright property and cannot be used without permission of the various owners.

THE COMPILERS.

Select Songs Nos. 1 and 2 will be bound up in one volume for those who desire it. This edition will be as complete a manual of praise as can be obtained, for use in the Prayer Meeting, the Sunday School, and the meetings of the Society of Christian Endeavor. Price, in cloth, $70.00 per 100 copies, by express; 85 cents each by mail.

SELECT SONGS, NO. 2.

No. 1. Grace before Meals.
WM. B. BRADBURY.

1. With Thy gifts Thy grace bestow, Feed our souls with heav'n-ly food,
2. In the strength which Thou dost give, Help us, Lord, henceforth to live,

Help us wor-thi-ly to show Grat-i-tude for ev-'ry good.
Make us know Thy per-fect will— In our lives Thy life ful-fill.

* As used by the Boston Superintendent's Union at their suppers.

2.   **FOR "GRACE."**
Tune—OLD HUNDRED.
(Before meals at sociables and public gatherings.)

1 Be present at our table, Lord;
  Be here and everywhere adored;
  These mercies bless, and grant that we
  May feast in Paradise with Thee.

2 We thank thee, Lord, for this our food,
  But more because of Jesus' blood;
  Let manna to our souls be given,
  The bread of life send down from heaven.
John Cennick.

3.   **CLOSING HYMN.**
Tune—GREENVILLE.

1 Come, Thou soul-transforming Spirit,
  Bless the sower and the seed;
  Let each heart Thy grace inherit;
  Raise the weak, the hungry feed;
    From the gospel
  Now supply Thy people's need.

2 Oh, may all enjoy the blessing
  Which Thy word's designed to give;
  Let us all Thy love possessing,
  Joyfully the truth receive,
    And forever
  To Thy praise and glory live.
Jonathan Evans, 1784.

4.   Sentence. (Gloria Tibi.)

Glo - ry, glo - ry, glo - ry be to Thee, O Lord!

Opening and Closing.

5. Gloria Patri.

CHARLES MEINEKE.

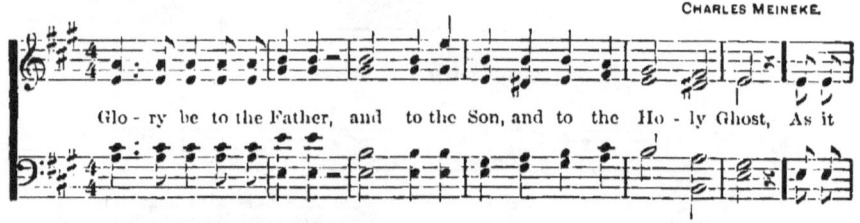
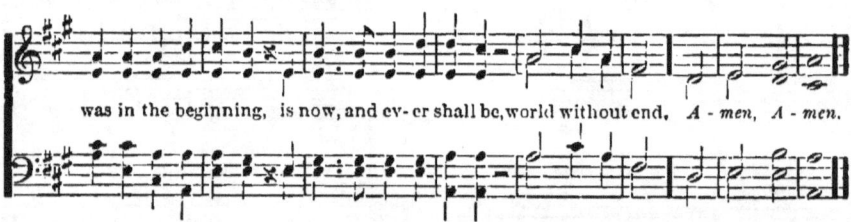

Glo - ry be to the Father, and to the Son, and to the Ho - ly Ghost, As it was in the beginning, is now, and ev-er shall be, world without end. A - men, A - men.

6. Gloria Patri.

HENRY W. GREATOREX.

Glo - ry be to the Father, and to the Son, and to the Ho - ly Ghost; As it was in the beginning, is now, and ev-er shall be, world without end. A - men, A - men.

Used by Arr. with Oliver Ditson Co., owners of Copyright.

7. Sentence. (Kyrie Eleison.)

CHAS. GOUNOD.

8. O Most Merciful. (Closing.)

R. HEBER.

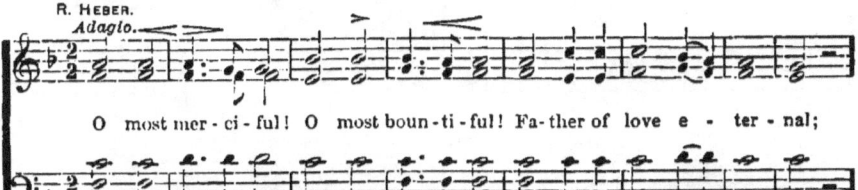

Opening and Closing.

9. O, Praise ye the Father.

JOHN F. GENUNG.   MARCANTOINE SIMAO.

Voices in Unison.

O, praise ye the Father, whose love supreme upholds us, Oh, praise ye the Son by ransomed mil-lions adored; Oh, praise ye the Spirit, whose guiding care enfolds us; For grace unseen, un-end-ing, Our life from ills de-fend-ing, To a-ges, of a-ges, oh, praise ye the Lord!

Opening and Closing.

10. Jesus, King of Glory.

W. H. Davison.

1. Je-sus, King of glo-ry Thron'd a-bove the sky, Je-sus, ten-der Sav-iour, Hear Thy chil-dren cry. Par-don our trans-gres-sions, Cleanse us from our sin, By Thy Spir-it help us Heav'nly life to win.
2. On this day of glad-ness, Bend-ing low the knee In Thine earthly tem-ple, Lord, we wor-ship Thee; Cel-e-brate Thy good-ness, Mer-cy, grace, and truth, All Thy lov-ing guid-ance Of our heed-less youth.
3. When the shadows lengthen, Show us, Lord, Thy way; Thro' the darkness lead us To the heav'nly day. When our course is fin-ished End-ed all the strife, Grant us with the faith-ful Palms and crowns of life.

REFRAIN.
Je-sus, King of glo-ry, Throned a-bove the sky, Je-sus, ten-der Sav-iour, Hear Thy chil-dren cry.

By permission from the "Church Hymnary."

Opening and Closing.

11.   The Lord be with us.

Rev. J. Ellerton.   Wm. B. Bradbury.

1. The Lord be with us as we bend His bless-ing to re-ceive; His gift of peace up-on us send, Be-fore His courts we leave. The Lord be with us as we walk A-long our homeward road; In silent thought or friendly talk Our hearts be still with God.

2. The Lord be with us till the night Shall close the day of rest; Be He of ev-'ry heart the Light, Of ev-'ry home the Guest. The Lord be with us as we bend His bless-ing to re-ceive; His gift of peace up-on us send, Be-fore His courts we leave.

Copyright, 1859, 1887, in Oriola, by W. B. Bradbury.

12.

1 The twilight falls, the night is near,
   I fold my work away,
  And kneel to One who bends to hear
   The story of the day.
  The old, old story; yet I kneel
   To tell it at Thy call,
  And cares grow lighter as I feel
   That Jesus knows them all.

2 Thou knowest all: I lean my head;
   My weary eyelids close;
  Content and glad awhile to tread
   This path, since Jesus knows.

And He has loved me: All my heart
   With answering love is stirred,
And every anguished pain and smart
   Finds healing in the word.

3 So here I lay me down to rest,
   As nightly shadows fall,
  And lean confiding on His breast
   Who knows and pities all.
  The twilight falls, the night is near,
   I fold my work away,
  And kneel to One who bends to hear
   The story of the day.
                   Unknown Author.

Opening and Closing.

14. Evening Prayer.

J. EDMESTON. GEO. C. STEBBINS.

1. Sav-iour, breathe an even-ing bless-ing, Ere re-pose our spir-its seal;
2. Tho' de-struc-tion walk a-round us, Tho' the ar-rows past us fly;
3. Tho' the night be dark and drear-y, Dark-ness can-not hide from Thee;
4. Should swift death this night o'er-take us, And our couch be-come our tomb,

Sin and want we come con-fess-ing, Thou canst save and Thou canst heal.
An-gel-guards from Thee sur-round us, We are safe if Thou art nigh.
Thou art He who, nev-er wea-ry, Watch-est where Thy peo-ple be.
May the morn in heav'n a-wake us, Clad in bright and death-less bloom.

Copyright, 1878, by Geo. C. Stebbins. Used by per.

15. Ere I Sleep.

JOHN CENNICK, 1742. C. DARNTON.

1. Ere I sleep, for ev-'ry fa-vor This day showed By my God,
2. Leave me not but ev-er love me; Let Thy peace Be my bliss

I will bless my Sav-iour.
Till Thou hence re-move me.

3 Thou, my Rock, my Guard, my Tower,
   Safely keep,
   While I sleep,
Me, with all Thy power.

4 And whene'er in death I slumber
   Let me rise
   With the wise,
Counted in their number.

Opening and Closing.

17. Praise the Rock of our Salvation.

FANNY J. CROSBY. HUBERT P. MAIN.

1. Praise the Rock of our sal-va-tion, Praise the might-y God a-bove;
2. Je-sus' blood so free-ly of-fer'd, Je-sus' blood a-vails for sin;
3. Praise the Rock of our sal-va-tion; Catch from yon-der ra-diant clime,

Come be-fore His sa-cred pres-ence With a grate-ful song of love.
Je-sus at the door of mer-cy, Waits to let the wand'rer in.
Strains by ev-er-last-ing a-ges, Ech-oed back in tones sub-lime.

CHORUS.

Hal-le-lu-jah! Hal-le-lu-jah! He is God, and He a-lone;
Wake the song of ad-o-ra-tion, Come with joy be-fore His throne.

Copyright, 1873, by Biglow & Main.

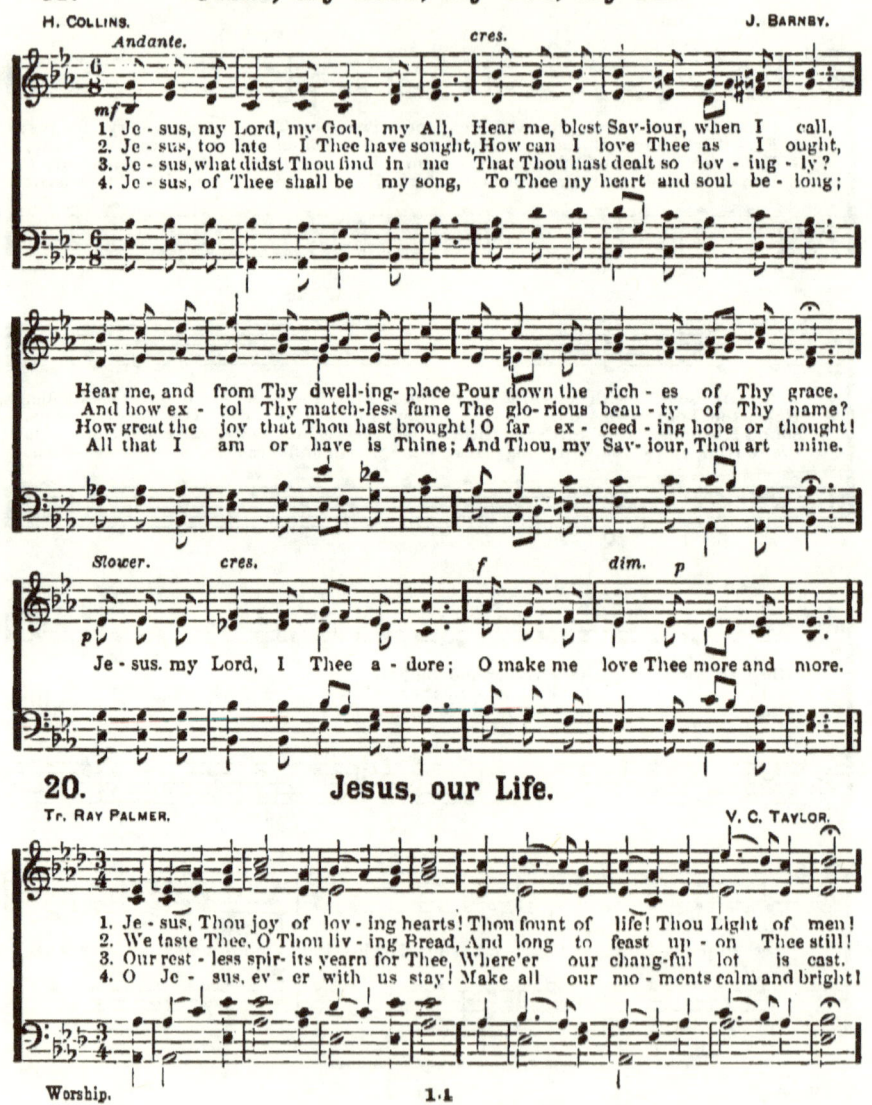

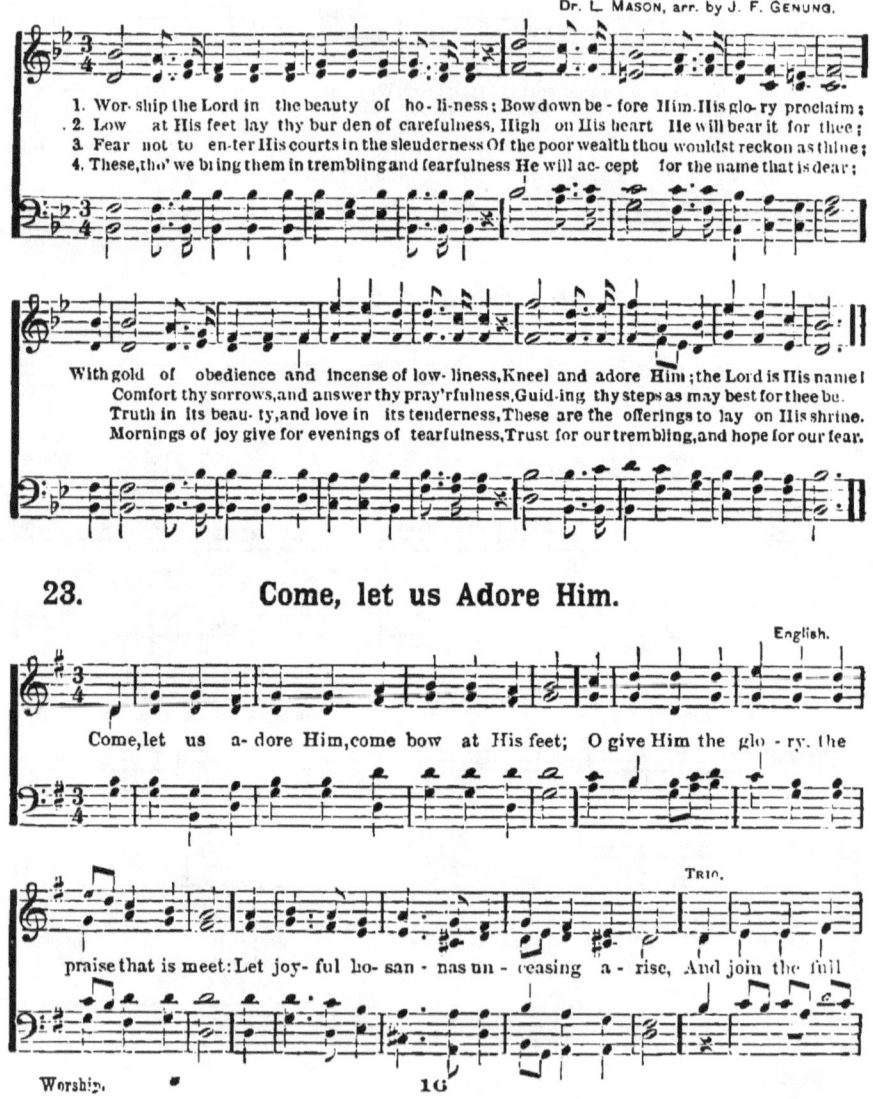

Come, let us Adore Him.—Concluded.

CHORUS

cho-rus that gladdens the skies, And join the full cho-rus that glad-dens the skies.

24. O had I Wings like a Dove.

C. J.
CHARLES JEFFEREYS.

1. O had I wings like a dove, I would fly A-way from this world of care;
2. O is it not writ-ten, Be-lieve and live? The heart by bright hope allured

My soul would mount to the realms on high, And seek for a ref-uge there;
Shall find the com-fort those words can give, And be by its faith as-sured;

D. S.—No fa-vored spot where con-tent has birth, In which I may find a rest?
D. S.—The light of re-lig-ion to guide us on In joy to the paths of heaven.

But is there no hav-en here on earth? No hope for the wounded breast?
Then why should we fear the cold world's frown, When truth to the heart has given;

Worship.

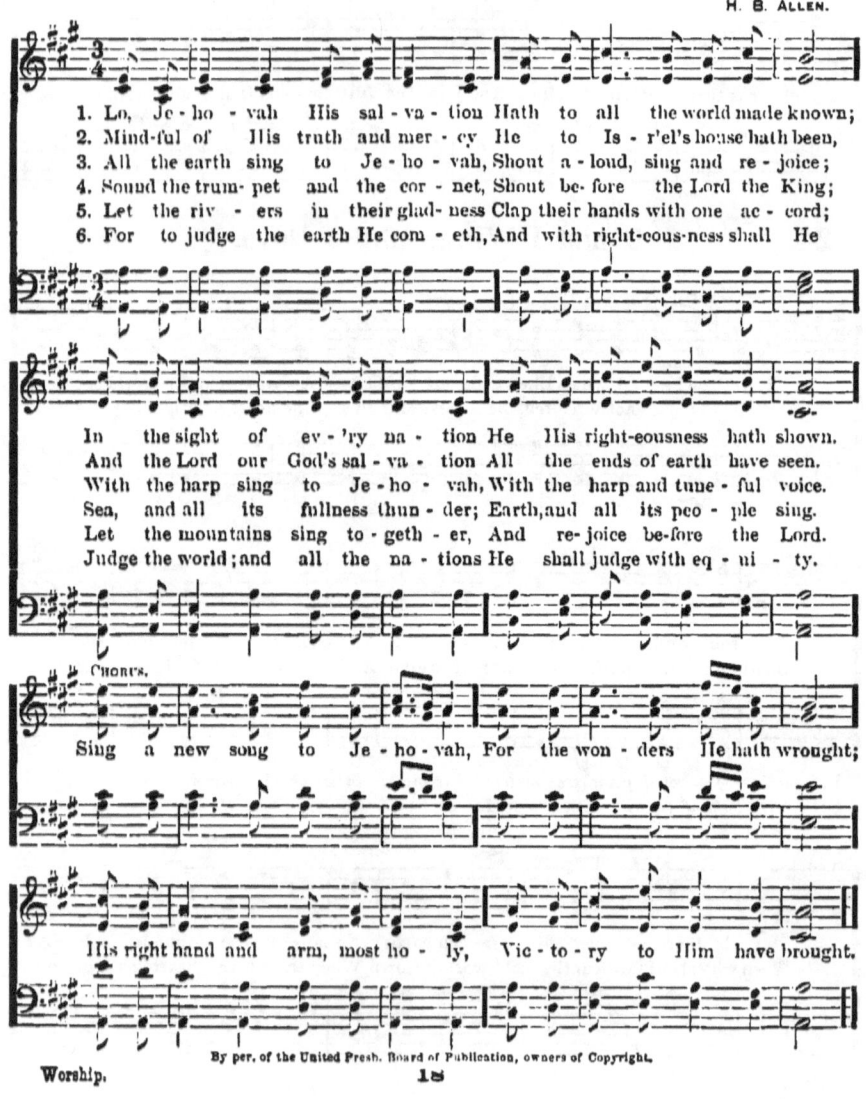

26.

1 Hark! the sound of angel-voices
  Over Bethlehem's star-lit plain;
  Hark! the heavenly host rejoices,
    Jesus comes on earth to reign.

CHO.—Sing a new song to Jehovah,
  For the wonders He hath wrought;
  His right hand and arm, most holy,
    Victory to Him have brought.

2 See celestial radiance beaming,
  Lighting up the midnight sky;
  'Tis the promised day-star gleaming,
    'Tis the day-spring from on high.

3 Angels from the realms of glory,
  Peace on earth delight to sing;
  Christian, tell the wondrous story,
    Go proclaim the Saviour King!
        C. Wordsworth.

27. My God, I Thank Thee.

ADELAIDE ANNE PROCTER.   German.

1. My God, I thank Thee, who hast made The earth so bright;
   So full of splen-dor and of joy. Beau-ty and light;
   So many glo-rious things are here so no-ble and right,

2. I thank Thee, too, that Thou hast made Joy to a-bound;
   So ma-ny gen-tle thoughts and deeds Cir-cling us round;
   That in the dark-est spot of earth some love is found.

3. I thank Thee more that all our joy Is touched with pain;
   That shad-ows fall on bright-est hours, That thorns re-main;
   So that earth's bliss may be our guide, and not our chain.

4 I thank Thee, Lord, that Thou hast kept
    The best in store;
  We have enough, yet not too much,
    To long for more;
  A yearning for a deeper peace
    Not known before.

5 I thank Thee, Lord, that here our souls
    Though amply blest,
  Can never find, although they seek
    A perfect rest;
  Nor ever shall, until they lean
    On Jesus' breast.

Worship.

30. Praise Him.

Fanny J. Crosby.   Chester G. Allen.

1. Praise Him! praise Him! Je-sus, our blessed Re-deem-er! Sing, O earth—His
2. Praise Him! praise Him! Je-sus, our blessed Re-deem-er! For our sins He

won-der-ful love pro-claim! Hail Him! hail Him! high-est arch-an-gels in
suf-fer'd, and bled, and died; He our Rock, our hope of e-ter-nal sal-

D. S.—*Praise Him! praise Him! tell of His ex-cel-lent*

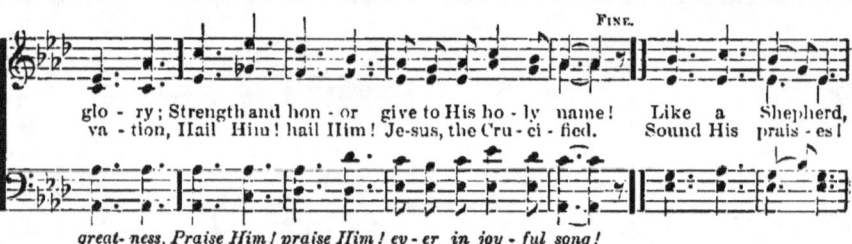

glo-ry; Strength and hon-or give to His ho-ly name! Like a Shepherd,
va-tion, Hail Him! hail Him! Je-sus, the Cru-ci-fied. Sound His prais-es!

great-ness, Praise Him! praise Him! ev-er in joy-ful song!

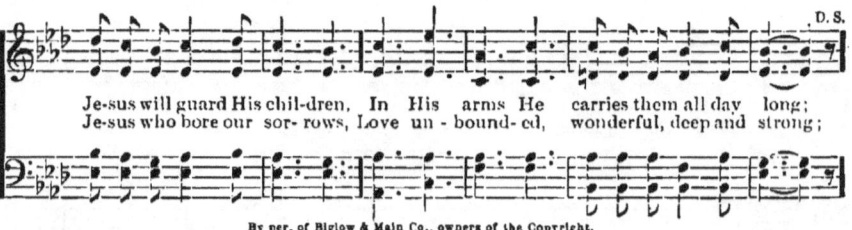

Je-sus will guard His chil-dren, In His arms He carries them all day long;
Je-sus who bore our sor-rows, Love un-bound-ed, wonderful, deep and strong;

By per. of Biglow & Main Co., owners of the Copyright.

31. Give Thanks.

E. O. BUTTERFIELD.

1. God's might-y works who can ex-press? Or show forth all His praise?
2. Re-mem-ber me, O Lord, with love, Which Thou to Thine dost bear;
3. That I Thy cho-sen's good may see, And in their joy re-joice;
4. We with our fa-thers have transgressed, And done in-i-qui-ty;
5. The won-ders great, which Thou, O Lord, Didst work in E-gypt land,

O blest are they that judg-ment keep, And just-ly do al-ways.
With Thy sal-va-tion, O my God, To vis-it me draw near.
And may with Thine in-her-it-ance Ex-ult with cheer-ful voice.
With them we have transgress-ors been, We have done wick-ed-ly.
Our fa-thers, though they saw, yet them They did not un-der-stand.

CHORUS.
Praise ye . . . . the Lord . . . His mer-cy shall en-
Praise ye the Lord, and give Him thanks, For bounti-ful is He; His ten-der mer-cy

dure, . . .
shall en-dure To all e-ter-ni-ty.

6 And they Thy mercies' multitude
  Kept not in memory;
  But at the sea, ev'n the Red sea,
  Provoked Him grievously.

7 Yet notwithstanding He then saved,
  Ev'n for His own name's sake;
  That so He might, to be well known,
  His mighty power make.

By per. of the United Presb. Board of Publication, owners of Copyright.

32. Oh, Praise the Lord.

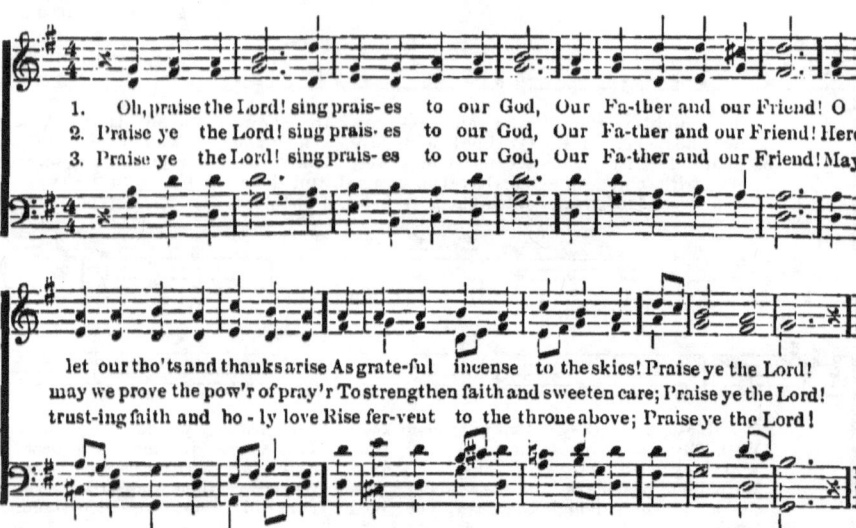

1. Oh, praise the Lord! sing prais-es to our God, Our Fa-ther and our Friend! O let our tho'ts and thanks arise As grate-ful incense to the skies! Praise ye the Lord!
2. Praise ye the Lord! sing prais-es to our God, Our Fa-ther and our Friend! Here may we prove the pow'r of pray'r To strengthen faith and sweeten care; Praise ye the Lord!
3. Praise ye the Lord! sing prais-es to our God, Our Fa-ther and our Friend! May trust-ing faith and ho-ly love Rise fer-vent to the throne above; Praise ye the Lord!

33. Pray, Always Pray.

Rev. E. H. BICKERSTETH.   G. R. CALDBECK.

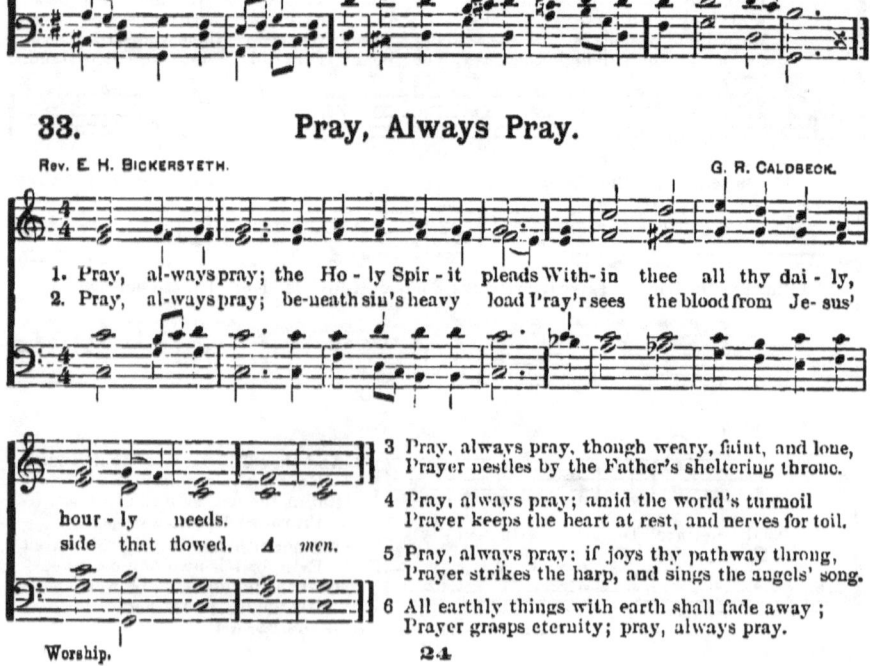

1. Pray, al-ways pray; the Ho-ly Spir-it pleads With-in thee all thy dai-ly, hour-ly needs.
2. Pray, al-ways pray; be-neath sin's heavy load Pray'r sees the blood from Je-sus' side that flowed. A men.

3 Pray, always pray, though weary, faint, and lone,
  Prayer nestles by the Father's sheltering throne.

4 Pray, always pray; amid the world's turmoil
  Prayer keeps the heart at rest, and nerves for toil.

5 Pray, always pray; if joys thy pathway throng,
  Prayer strikes the harp, and sings the angels' song.

6 All earthly things with earth shall fade away;
  Prayer grasps eternity; pray, always pray.

Worship.

34. Sweetly Dawns the Sabbath Morning.

THOS. B. STEPHENSON, D. D.   WM. B. BRADBURY

1. Sweetly dawns the Sabbath morn-ing On the world so full of care;
2. 'Tis the day when man's Re-deem-er Rose tri-umph-ant o'er the grave;
3. 'Tis the day whose rest and glad-ness Show what all my life should be;
4. 'Tis the day whose calm, so ho-ly, Shadows forth the bet-ter rest,

Bidding man for-get his la-bor, Call-ing to the house of prayer.
Sealing thus His work com-plet-ed, Tell-ing thus His power to save.
Yielding all by faith to Je-sus, Find-ing Je-sus all to me.
Where the crown-ed saints are sing-ing With their Lord, su-premely blest.

Oh, sweet and strong, His saints a-mong, We sing to God our Sabbath song!
Then loud and long, to Christ so strong, To save the lost we raise our song,
Oh, how I long, in Christ made strong, To sing each day faith's Sabbath song!
'Twill not be long till 'mid that throng We sing th'e-ter-nal Sabbath song,

Our Sab-bath song, Our Sab-bath song, We raise to Christ our Sab-bath song.
Our Sab-bath song, Our Sab-bath song, We raise to Christ our Sab-bath song.
Faith's Sabbath song, Faith's Sabbath song, I'd sing each day faith's Sabbath song.
Heav'n's Sabbath song, Heav'n's Sabbath song, We'll sing th'e-ter-nal Sabbath song.

By per. The Biglow & Main Co., owners of Copyright.

Lord's Day.

39. O God, the Rock of Ages.

E. BICKERSTETH. HUBERT P. MAIN.

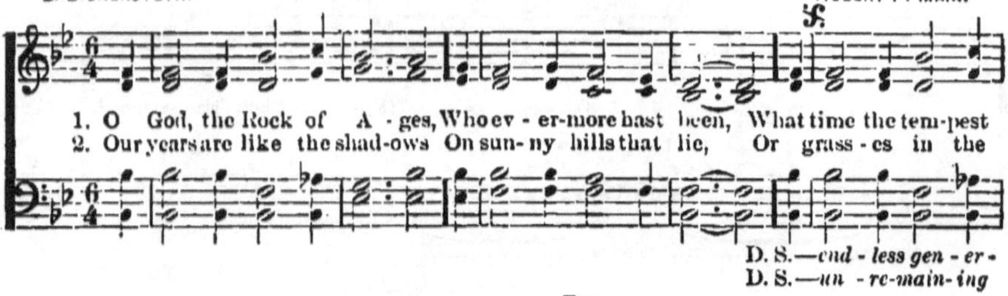

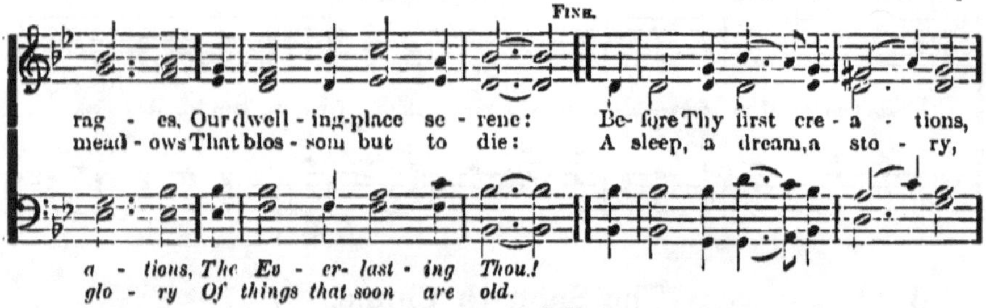

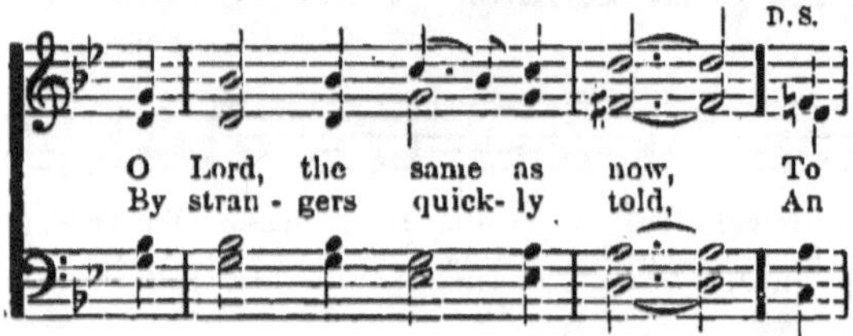

1. O God, the Rock of Ages, Whoever-more hast been, What time the tempest rages, Our dwelling-place serene: Before Thy first creations, The Everlasting Thou!
2. Our years are like the shadows On sunny hills that lie, Or grasses in the meadows That blossom but to die: A sleep, a dream, a story, By strangers quickly told, An unremaining glory Of things that soon are old.

D.S.—endless generations, The Everlasting Thou!
D.S.—unremaining glory Of things that soon are old.

O Lord, the same as now, To
By strangers quickly told, An

3. O Thou who canst not slumber,
   Whose light grows never pale,
   Teach us aright to number
   Our years before they fail;
   On us Thy mercy lighten,
   On us Thy goodness rest,
   And let Thy Spirit brighten
   The hearts Thyself hast blessed!

Copyright, 1893, by The Biglow & Main Co.

40. Father of Mercies.

P. DODDRIDGE. J. P. HOLBROOK.

1. Father of mercies! send Thy grace, All powerful from above,
2. Oh, may our sympathizing breasts The generous pleasure know,
3. On wings of love the Saviour flew, To raise us from the ground,

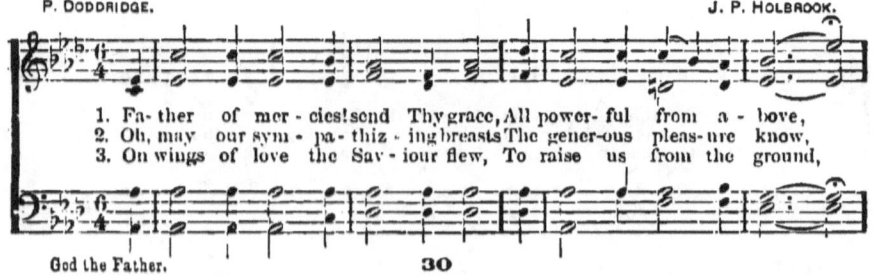

God the Father.

Father of Mercies.—Concluded.

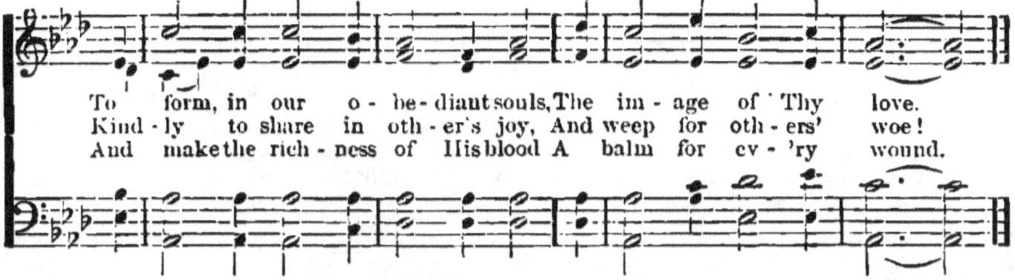

To form, in our o-be-dient souls, The im-age of Thy love.
Kind-ly to share in oth-er's joy, And weep for oth-ers' woe!
And make the rich-ness of His blood A balm for ev-'ry wound.

41. Angel Voices ever Singing.

FRANCIS POTT.   A. S. SULLIVAN.

1. An-gel voi-ces, ev-er sing-ing Round Thy throne of light—
2. Thou, who art be-yond the far-thest Mor-tal eye can scan,
3. Here, Great God, to-day we of-fer Of Thine own to Thee;

An-gel harps, for ev-er ring-ing, Rest not day nor night;
Can it be that Thou re-gard-est Songs of sin-ful man?
And for Thine ac-cept-ance prof-fer, All un-worth-i-ly,

Thous-ands on-ly live to bless Thee, And con-fess Thee, Lord of might!
Can we feel that Thou art near us And wilt hear us? Yea, we can.
Hearts and minds, and hands and voic-es, In our choic-est mel-o-dy.

God the Father.

43. I Cannot Always Trace the Way.

Sir John Bowring.   Lowell Mason.

1. I cannot always trace the way, Where Thou, almighty One, dost move, But I can always, always say, That God is love.
2. When fear her chilling mantle flings O'er earth, my soul to heav'n above, As to her native home, up-springs; For God is love.
3. When myst'ry clouds my darkened path, I'll check my dread, my doubts reprove; In this my soul sweet comfort hath, That God is love.
4. Oh, may this truth my heart employ, Bid ev'ry gloomy thought remove, And turn all tears, all woes to joy,—Thou, God art Love!

44.

1 Dear Saviour, while on earth I stray,
Be Thou my Shepherd, Thou my way;
And to the everlasting day,
   Abide with me!

2 In sickness, sorrow, anguish, woe,
In tribulation here below,
At home, abroad, where'er I go,
   Abide with me!

3 Be with me through the hours of night,
Be Thou my everlasting flight,
In leading me to mansions bright,
   Abide with me!

4 When wearied by fatigue, I sleep,
My soul, in mercy, Jesus, keep;
To guide and guard Thy helpless sheep,
   Abide with me!

5 And when on earth I breathe no more,
I'll praise Thee on the heavenly shore,
Then, Lord, Thou wilt for evermore
   Abide with me!

God the Father.

45.

1 My God, my Father, while I stray
Far from my home, on life's rough way,
O teach me from my heart to say,
   "Thy will be done!"

2 Though dark my path, and sad my lot,
Let me be still and murmur not,
Or breathe the prayer divinely taught,
   "Thy will be done!"

3 Let but my fainting heart be blest
With Thy sweet Spirit for its Guest,
My God, to Thee I leave the rest;
   "Thy will be done!"

4 Renew my will from day to day;
Blend it with Thine, and take away
All that now makes it hard to say
   "Thy will be done!"

5 Then, when on earth I breathe no more
The prayer oft mixed with tears before,
I'll sing upon a happier shore,
   "Thy will be done!"

Charlotte Elliott.

Blessed Night.—Concluded.

4 Thus revealed to shepherds' eyes,
Hidden from the great and wise,—
Entering earth in lowly guise—
Alleluia!

5 Entering by the narrow door,
Laid upon this rocky floor,
Placed in yonder manger poor.
Alleluia!

6 We adore Thee as our King,
And to Thee our song we sing;
Our best offering to Thee bring.
Alleluia!

7 Mighty King of Righteousness,
King of glory, King of Peace,
Never shall Thy kingdom cease!
Alleluia!

48. O little Town of Bethlehem.

PHILLIPS BROOKS, D. D.   LEWIS H. REDNER, by per.

1. O lit-tle town of Beth-lehem, How still we see thee lie! A-bove thy deep and dreamless sleep The si-lent stars go by; Yet in thy dark streets shin-eth The ev-er-lasting Light; The hopes and fears of all the years Are met in thee to-night!

2. For Christ is born of Ma-ry; And gath-er'd all a-bove, While mortals sleep, the an-gels keep Their watch of wond'ring love. O morn-ing stars! to-geth-er Pro-claim the ho-ly birth, And prais-es sing to God the King, And peace to men on earth!

3. How si-lent-ly, how si-lent-ly The wondrous gift is given! So God im-parts to hu-man hearts The blessings of His heav'n. No ear may hear His com-ing; But in this world of sin, Where meek souls will receive Him still, The dear Christ enters in.

4. O ho-ly Child of Beth-lehem, De-scend to us we pray; Cast out our sin and en-ter in.—Be born in us to-day! We hear the Christ-mas an-gels The great glad tidings tell,—Oh, come to us, a-bide with us, Our Lord Em-man-u-el!

Birth of Christ.

49. Softly the Night is Sleeping.

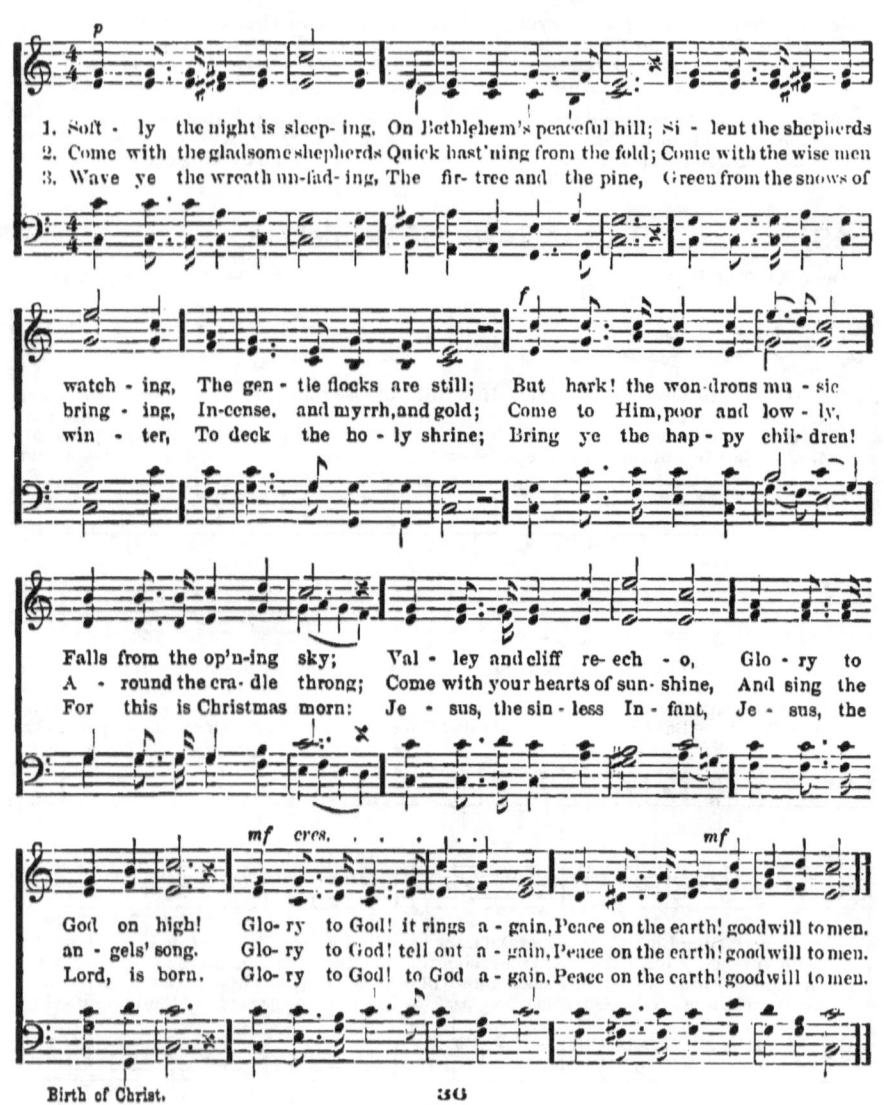

1. Soft-ly the night is sleep-ing, On Bethlehem's peaceful hill; Si-lent the shepherds watch-ing, The gen-tle flocks are still; But hark! the won-drous mu-sic Falls from the op'n-ing sky; Val-ley and cliff re-ech-o, Glo-ry to God on high! Glo-ry to God! it rings a-gain, Peace on the earth! goodwill to men.

2. Come with the gladsome shepherds Quick hast'ning from the fold; Come with the wise men bring-ing, In-cense, and myrrh, and gold; Come to Him, poor and low-ly, A-round the cra-dle throng; Come with your hearts of sun-shine, And sing the an-gels' song. Glo-ry to God! tell out a-gain, Peace on the earth! goodwill to men.

3. Wave ye the wreath un-fad-ing, The fir-tree and the pine, Green from the snows of win-ter, To deck the ho-ly shrine; Bring ye the hap-py chil-dren! For this is Christmas morn: Je-sus, the sin-less In-fant, Je-sus, the Lord, is born. Glo-ry to God! to God a-gain, Peace on the earth! goodwill to men.

Birth of Christ.

50. Hark, what Mean those Holy Voices.

JOHN CAWOOD.

1. Hark, what mean those ho-ly voi-ces, Sweetly sounding thro' the skies;
Lo, th' an-gel-ic host re-joic-es, Heav'nly al-le-lu-ias rise.
Lis-ten to the wondrous sto-ry, Which they chant in hymns of joy:
Glo-ry in the high-est, glo-ry; Glo-ry be to God most high.

2 Peace on earth, good-will from heaven,
  Reaching far as a man is found;
Souls redeemed, and sins forgiven,
  Loud our golden harps shall sound.
Christ is born, the great Anointed,
  Heaven and earth His glory sing;
O receive whom God appointed
  For your Prophet, Priest, and King.

3 Hasten, mortals, to adore Him;
  Learn His name, and taste His joy,
Till in heaven you sing before Him,
  Glory be to God most high.
Let us learn the wondrous story
  Of our great Redeemer's birth;
Spread the brightness of His glory,
  Till it cover all the earth.

Birth of Christ.

51. The Voice of the Christ-Child.

PHILLIPS BROOKS, D.D.   DAVENANT.

1. The earth has grown old with its bur-den of care But at Christ-mas it al-ways is young; And the soul of its mu-sic breaks forth on the air; When the song of the an-gels is sung. 2. It is com-ing old earth, it is com-ing to-night, On the snowflakes which cov-er thy sod, And the voice of the Christ-child tells

3. On the sad and the lone-ly the wretch-ed and poor, That voice of the Christ-child shall fall; And to ev-'ry blind wan-der-er o-pens the door, With a sunshine and welcome for all. 4. The feet of the humblest may walk in the field, Where the feet of the ho-liest have trod, And this is the mar-vel to

Birth of Christ.

The Voice of the Christ-Child.—Concluded.

out with de-light; That man-kind are the chil-dren of God.
mor-tals re-veal'd, That man-kind are the chil-dren of God.

52.

1 How sweet is the Bible! how pure is the light
  That streams from its pages divine!
'Tis a star that shines soft through the gloom
  of the night,
Of jewels a wonderful mine.
'Tis bread for the hungry, 'tis food for the
  poor,
A balm for the wretched and sad,—
'Tis the gift of a Father—His likeness is there,
And the hearts of His children are glad.

2 Oh teach me, blest Jesus, to seek for Thy face,
  To me let Thy welcome be given,
Now speak to my heart some kind message
  of grace,
And words that shall guide me to heaven.
How sweet is the Bible! how pure is the light
  That streams from its pages divine!
'Tis a star that shines soft through the gloom
  of the night,
Of jewels a wonderful mine.

53. Christ the Lord Comes Down To-night.

ALICE BROTHERTON.   HUBERT P. MAIN

1. Christ the Lord comes down to-night: Leaves His an-gels cloth'd in white,
2. Ev-'ry blow and ev-'ry frown, Sets a sharp thorn in His crown;
3. Do some lit-tle deed to-day That shall cheer His wea-ry way;
4. "Peace on earth, good-will to men," An-gels chant the strain a-gain,

Tak-ing up His Cross a-gain Walks in haunts of sin-ful men.
For each deed of Char-i-ty, A new star there-in shall be.
Say some kind word, breathe a pray'r, Help Him thus that Cross to bear!
In the song all souls u-nite: Christ the Lord comes down to-night.

Copyright, 1892, by Hubert P. Main.

Birth of Christ.

57. Memories of Galilee.

Rober. Morris, L.L.D. H. R. Palmer.

Used by permission of Dr. H. R. Palmer, owner of Copyright.

Memories of Galilee.—Concluded.

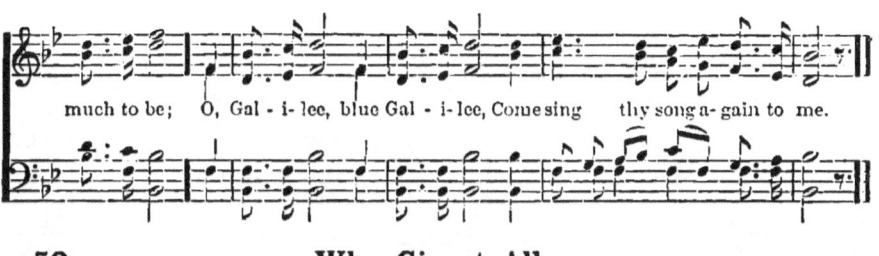

much to be; O, Gal-i-lee, blue Gal-i-lee, Come sing thy song a-gain to me.

58. Who Givest All.

GEO. RAWSON.   Rev. J. B. DYKES.

1. O Lord of Heav'n, and earth, and sea, To Thee all praise and glo - ry be;
2. Thou didst not spare Thine on - ly Son, But gav'st Him for a world un - done,
3. Thou giv'st the Spir - it's bless-ed dow'r, Spir-it of life, and love, and pow'r,
4. For souls re-deem'd, for sins for-giv'n, For means of grace, and hopes of Heav'n,
5. To Thee, from whom we all de-rive Our life, our gifts, our pow'r to give;

How shall we show our love to Thee, Who giv - est all?
And free - ly with that bless - ed One Thou giv - est all.
And dost His sev'n - fold gra - ces show'r Up - on us all.
What can to Thee, O Lord, be giv'n, Who giv - est all?
O may we ev - er with Thee live, Who giv - est all!

59.

1 By Christ redeemed, in Christ restored,
   We keep the memory adored,
   And show the death of our dear Lord,
      Until He come.

2 His body broken in our stead
   Is here, in this memorial bread;
   And so our feeble love is fed,
      Until He come.

3 His fearful drops of agony,
   His life-blood shed for us we see
   The wine shall tell the mystery,
      Until He come.

4 Oh, blessèd hope! with this elate,
   Let not our hopes be desolate,
   But, strong in faith, in patience wait,
      Until He come.

                    Christopher Wordsworth, 1863.

Life of Christ.

Sunshine in the Soul.—Concluded.

When Je-sus shows His smil-ing face, There is sunshine in my soul.

61. Thy Ways are Beautiful.

LISA A. FLETCHER.   HUBERT P. MAIN.

1. Thy ways are beau-ti-ful, Thy paths are peace, My God and King!
2. Thy love is sweet, and fills My emp-ty soul, My Lord and Light!
3. Thy pres-ence is the Star Which leads the way, My Sav-iour dear!

For oft Thou bidd'st the rag-ing tu-mult cease,
I will not fear tho' seas of sor-row roll—
E'en tho' I see one on-ly glim-m'ring ray—

Thou bidd'st the rag-ing tu-mult cease, And faith to sing.
Not fear tho' seas of sor-row roll, Nor shrink from night.
E'en tho' one on-ly glim-m'ring ray, I know thou'rt near.

Copyright, 1893, by The Biglow & Main Co.

Life of Christ.

The Strife is O'er.—Concluded.

The song of tri-umph has be-gun; Hal-le-lu-jah!
All glo-ry to our ris-en Head; Hal-le-lu-jah!
Let hymns of praise His tri-umphs tell. Hal-le-lu-jah!

64. Come, ye Faithful, Raise the Strain.

Rev. J. M. NEALE, tr.
GEO. J. ELVEY.

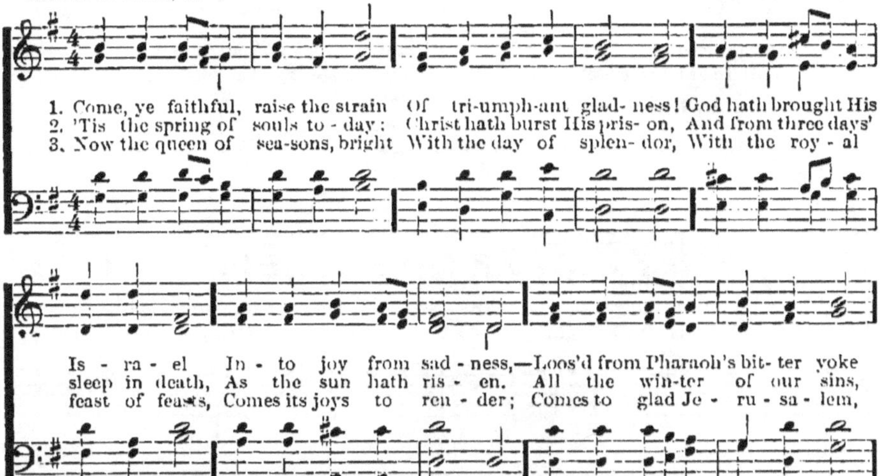

1. Come, ye faithful, raise the strain Of tri-umph-ant glad-ness! God hath brought His
2. 'Tis the spring of souls to-day: Christ hath burst His pris-on, And from three days'
3. Now the queen of sea-sons, bright With the day of splen-dor, With the roy-al

Is - ra - el In - to joy from sad-ness,—Loos'd from Pharaoh's bit-ter yoke
sleep in death, As the sun hath ris-en. All the win-ter of our sins,
feast of feasts, Comes its joys to ren-der; Comes to glad Je-ru-sa-lem,

Ja-cob's sons and daughters,—Led them with unmoisten'd feet Thro' the Red Sea wa-ters.
Long and dark, is fly-ing From His light to whom we give Laud and praise un-dy-ing.
Which, with true af-fec-tion, Welcomes in unwearied strains Je-sus' res-ur-rec-tion.

Resurrection of Christ.

Sound the High Praises of Jesus.—Concluded.

came and He conquer'd, His victo-ry sing, His vic-to-ry sing, His vic-to-ry sing!

66. Resurrection Song.

THE QUESTION.

C. F. HERNAMAN. A. REDHEAD.

1. Ear-ly, with blush of dawn, Speeding away, Shrouded in morning robes, Say, who are they?
2. See, in their hands they bear Spices most sweet: Whom are they hastening Ear-ly to greet?

THE ANSWER.

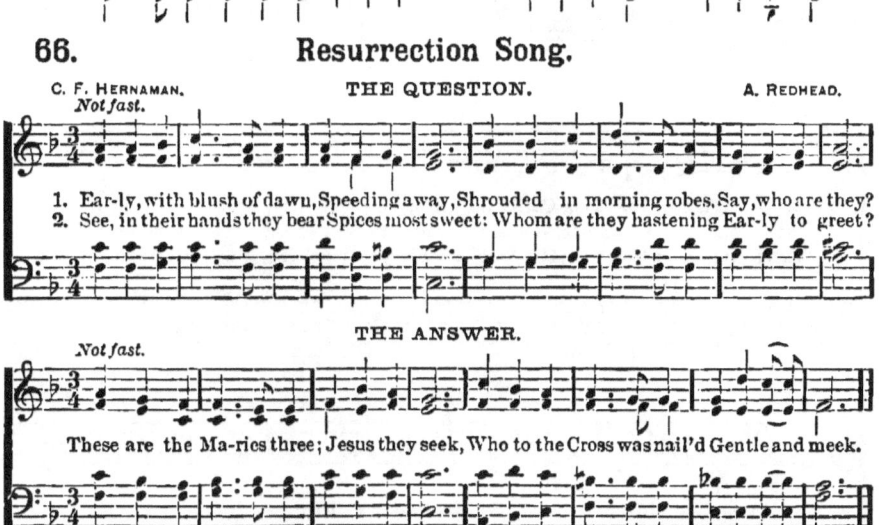

These are the Ma-ries three; Jesus they seek, Who to the Cross was nail'd Gentle and meek.

THE QUESTION.
Whose is that garden-fold,
Eager they seek,
Why that stone rolled away,
Baffling the weak?

THE ANSWER.
This is the garden-fold,
Wherein they laid,
Loving, His lifeless form,
Bold, yet not afraid.

THE QUESTION.
Why are they pausing now,
Close by the cave?
Whom are they seeking for
In the dark grave?

THE ANSWER.

1 Trembling, they now behold
  Where He had lain,
Clothed in shining robes,
  Bright angels twain.

2 Hark! they are speaking now—
  "Fear not," they say;
"Whom you are seeking here
  Is risen to-day!"

By two Classes, or the School in two Divisions.
Resurrection of Christ.

67. Golden Harps are Sounding.

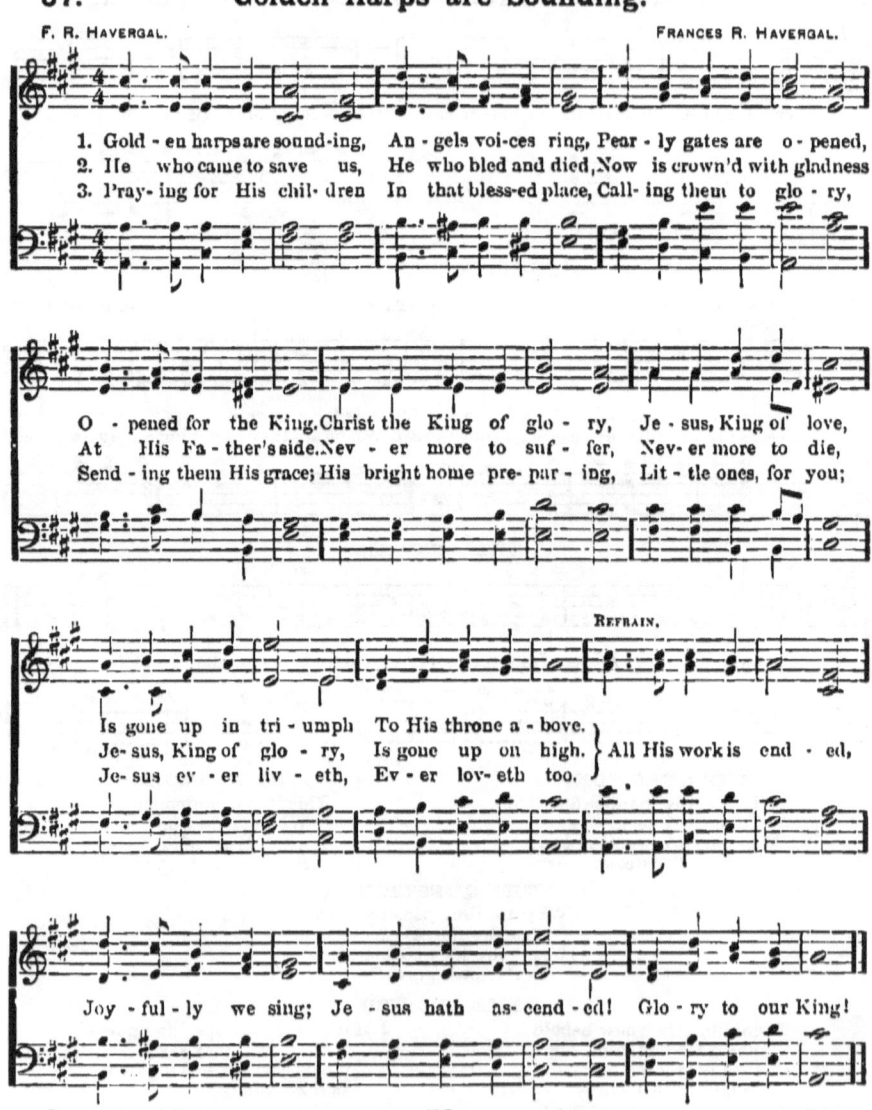

Resurrection of Christ.

68. Shine on, O Star!

VICTORIA STUART. IRA D. SANKEY.

1. Shine on, O Star of beau-ty, Thou Christ enthroned a-bove;
   Re-flect-ing in Thy bright-ness, Our Fa-ther's look of love.
2. Shine on, O Star of glo-ry, We lift our eyes to Thee;
   Be-yond the clouds that gath-er, Thy ra-diant light we see.
3. Shine on, O Star un-chang-ing, And guide our pil-grim way,
   Un-til we see the dawn-ing Of heav'n's e-ter-nal day.
4. And when, with Thy re-deem'd ones, We reach the heav-'nly shore,
   May we with Thee in glo-ry Shine on for-ev-er-more.

CHORUS.

Shine on, shine on, shine on, shine on, Thou bright and beau-ti-ful Star, shine on;
Shine on, shine on, shine on;
shine on, beau-ti-ful Star
Shine on, shine on, shine on, Thou bright and beau-ti-ful Star, shine on.
Shine on, shine on, *rit.*

Copyright, 1886, by Ira D. Sankey.

Adoration of Christ.

4 Weak is the effort of my heart,
And cold my warmest thought,
But when I see Thee as Thou art,
I'll praise Thee as I ought.

5 Till then I would Thy love proclaim
With every fleeting breath,
And may the music of Thy name
Refresh my soul in death.

Adoration of Christ.

Sing of Jesus, Sing Forever.—Concluded.

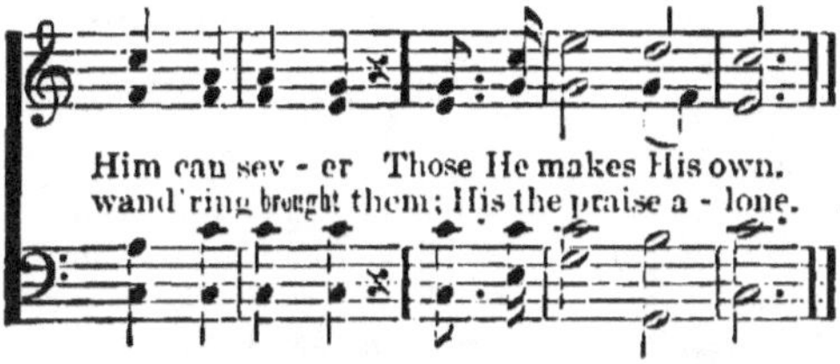

3 Through the desert Jesus leads them,
With the bread of heaven He feeds them,
And thro' all the way He speeds them
To their home above.

4 There they see the Lord who bought them,
Him who came from heaven, and sought them,
Him who by His spirit taught them,
Him they serve and love.

71. Light of the World, We Hail Thee.

JOHN S. B. MONSELL.   V. BELLINI.

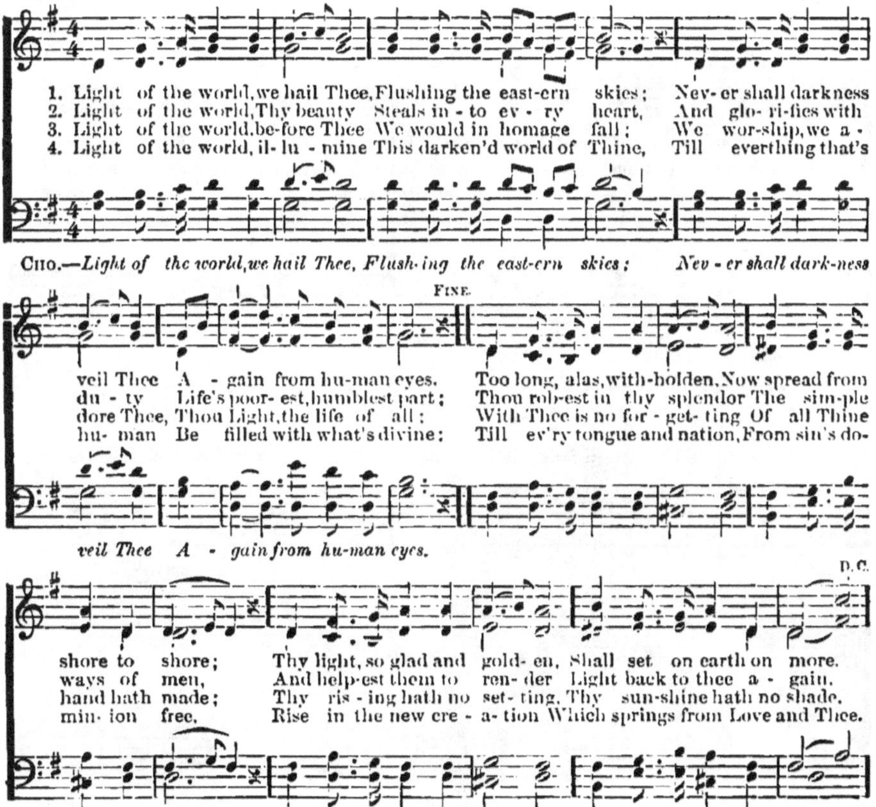

1. Light of the world, we hail Thee, Flushing the east-ern skies; Nev-er shall darkness veil Thee A-gain from hu-man eyes. Too long, alas, with-holden, Now spread from shore to shore; Thy light, so glad and gold-en, Shall set on earth no more.
2. Light of the world, Thy beauty Steals in-to ev-ry heart, And glo-ri-fies with du-ty Life's poor-est, humblest part; Thou rob-est in thy splendor The sim-ple ways of men, And help-est them to ren-der Light back to thee a-gain.
3. Light of the world, be-fore Thee We would in homage fall; We wor-ship, we a-dore Thee, Thou Light, the life of all; With Thee is no for-get-ting Of all Thine hand hath made; Thy ris-ing hath no set-ting, Thy sun-shine hath no shade.
4. Light of the world, il-lu-mine This darken'd world of Thine, Till everything that's hu-man Be filled with what's divine; Till ev'ry tongue and nation, From sin's do-min-ion free, Rise in the new cre-a-tion Which springs from Love and Thee.

CHO.—Light of the world, we hail Thee, Flush-ing the east-ern skies; Nev-er shall dark-ness veil Thee A-gain from hu-man eyes.

Adoration of Christ.

72. Children of Jerusalem.

JOHN HENLEY. English Melody.

1. Chil-dren of Je-ru-sa-lem Sang the praise of Jesus' name;
   Chil-dren too of mod-ern days, Join to sing the Saviour's praise.
2. We have oft-en heard and read What the roy-al psalm-ist said,
   Babes and suck-lings' art-less lays, Shall pro-claim the Saviour's praise.
3. We are taught to love the Lord; We are taught to read His word;
   We are taught the way to heaven: Praise for all to God be given!
4. Par-ents, teach-ers, old and young, All u-nite to swell the song:
   High-er and yet high-er rise, Till ho-san-nas reach the skies.

CHORUS.

Hark! hark! hark! while in-fant voic-es sing, Hark! hark! hark! while in-fant voices sing
Loud ho-san-nas, loud ho-san-nas, loud ho-san-nas to our King.

Adoration of Christ.

73. O Morning Star!

C. Winkworth, tr.   P. Nicolai.

1. O Morning Star! how fair and bright Thou beam-est forth in trust and light! O Sov-'reign meek and low - ly, Thou Root of Jes-se, David's Son, My Lord and Bridegroom, Thou hast won My heart to serve Thee sole - ly! Ho - ly art Thou, fair and glorious, All vic - to- rious, rich in bless - ing, Rule and might o'er all pos - sess - ing.
2. Thou heav'nly Brightness! Light Divine! O deep with - in my heart now shine, And make Thee there an al - tar! Fill me with joy and strength to be Thy member, ev - er join'd to Thee In love that can- not fal - ter; Tow'rd Thee longing doth possess me, Turn and bless me; for Thy glad - ness Eye and heart here pine in sad - ness.
3. But if Thou look on me in love, There straightway falls from God a-bove A ray of pur - est pleas-ure; Thy word and spirit, flesh and blood, Refresh my soul with heav-enly food, Thou art my hid-den treas -ure; Let Thy grace, Lord, warm and cheer me, O draw near me; Thou hast taught us Thee to seek since Thou hast sought us!
4. Here will I rest, and hold it fast, The Lord I love is first and last. The end as the be - gin - ning! Here I can calm-ly die, for Thou Wilt raise me where Thou dwell-est now, A - bove all tears, all sin - ning: A-men! A- men! come, Lord Jesus, Soon re - lease us, with deep yearn - ing, Lord we look for Thy re - turn - ing!

Adoration of Christ.

75. O Spirit of the Living God.

JANE E. BROWNE.   S. S. WESLEY.

1. O Spirit of the liv-ing God, Brooding with dove-like wings O-ver the helpless
and the weak A-mong cre-a-ted things!

2. Where should our feebleness find strength, Our helplessness a stay, Didst Thou not bring us strength, and help, And comfort, day by day?

3 Great are Thy consolations, Lord,
   And mighty is Thy power,
In sickness and in solitude,
   In sorrow's darkest hour.

4 O, if the souls that now despise
   And grieve Thee, heavenly Dove,
Would seek Thee, and would welcome Thee,
   How would they prize Thy love!

76. Come, Holy Ghost, in Love

Tr. by RAY PALMER, D.D.   LOWELL MASON.

1. Come, Ho-ly Ghost, in love Shed on us from a-bove Thine own bright ray! Di-vine-ly good Thou art; Thy sa-cred gifts impart To gladden each sad heart: Oh, come to-day!

2. Come, tend'rest friend, and best, Our most delightful guest, With soothing pow'r; Rest, which the wea-ry know, Shade, 'mid the noontide glow, Peace, when deep griefs o'erflow, Cheer us this hour!

3. Come, light se-rene, and still Our in-most bosoms fill; Dwell in each breast: We know no dawn but Thine; Send forth Thy beams divine, On our dark souls to shine, And make us blest!

4. Come, all the faithful bless; Let all, who Christ confess, His praise employ; Give virtue's rich reward; Vic-to-rious death accord, And, with our glorious Lord, E-ter-nal joy!

Holy Spirit.

77. Book of Grace and Glory.

THOS. MACKELLAR. LOWELL MASON.

1. Book of grace, and book of glo-ry, Gift of God to age and youth,
2. Book of love! in ac-cents ten-der Speak-ing un-to such as we;
3. Book of peace! when nights of sor-row Fall up-on us drear-i-ly,
4. Book of life! when we, re-pos-ing, Bid fare-well to friends we love,

Won-drous is Thy sa-cred sto-ry, Bright, bright, with truth.
May it lead us, Lord, to ren-der All, all to Thee.
Thou wilt bring a shin-ing mor-row, Full, full of Thee.
Give us, for the life then clos-ing, Life, life a-bove.

78.

1 Star of peace, to wanderers weary,
　Bright the beams that smile on me,
　Cheer the pilot's vision dreary,
　　Far, far at sea.

2 Star of hope, gleam on the billow,
　Bless the soul that sighs for Thee,
　Bless the sailor's lonely pillow,
　　Far, far at sea.

3 Star of faith, when winds are mocking
　All his toil, he flies to Thee;
　Save him, on the billows rocking,
　　Far, far at sea.

4 Star divine, O safely guide him,
　Bring the wanderer home to Thee;
　Sore temptations long have tried him,
　　Far, far at sea.

J. C. B. Simpson.

Scriptures.

82. Thy Word is like a Deep Mine.

CHAS. F. ROPER.

1. Thy Word is like a deep, deep mine, And jew-els rich and rare,
2. Thy Word is like a star-ry host, A thous-and rays of light
3. Thy Word is like a glo-rious choir, And loud its an-thems ring,
4. Thy Word is like an ar-mor-y, Where sol-diers may re-pair,

Are hid-den in its might-y depths, For ev-'ry search-er there.
Are seen to guide the trav-el-er, And make His path-way bright.
Though ma-ny tongues and parts u-nite, It is one song they sing.
And find for life's long bat-tle-day, All need-ful weap-ons there.

83. Lord, Thy Word Abideth.

Rev. H. W. BAKER.   W. BOYD.

1. Lord, Thy word a-bid-eth, And our foot-steps guid-eth; Who its truth be-liev-eth Light and joy re-ceiv-eth.
2. When the storms are o'er us, And dark clouds be-fore us, Then its light di-rect-eth, And our way pro-tect-eth.

3 Word of mercy, giving
Succor to the living;
Word of life supplying
Comfort to the dying!

4 Oh, that we, discerning
Its most holy learning,
Lord, may love and fear Thee,
Evermore be near Thee!

Scriptures.

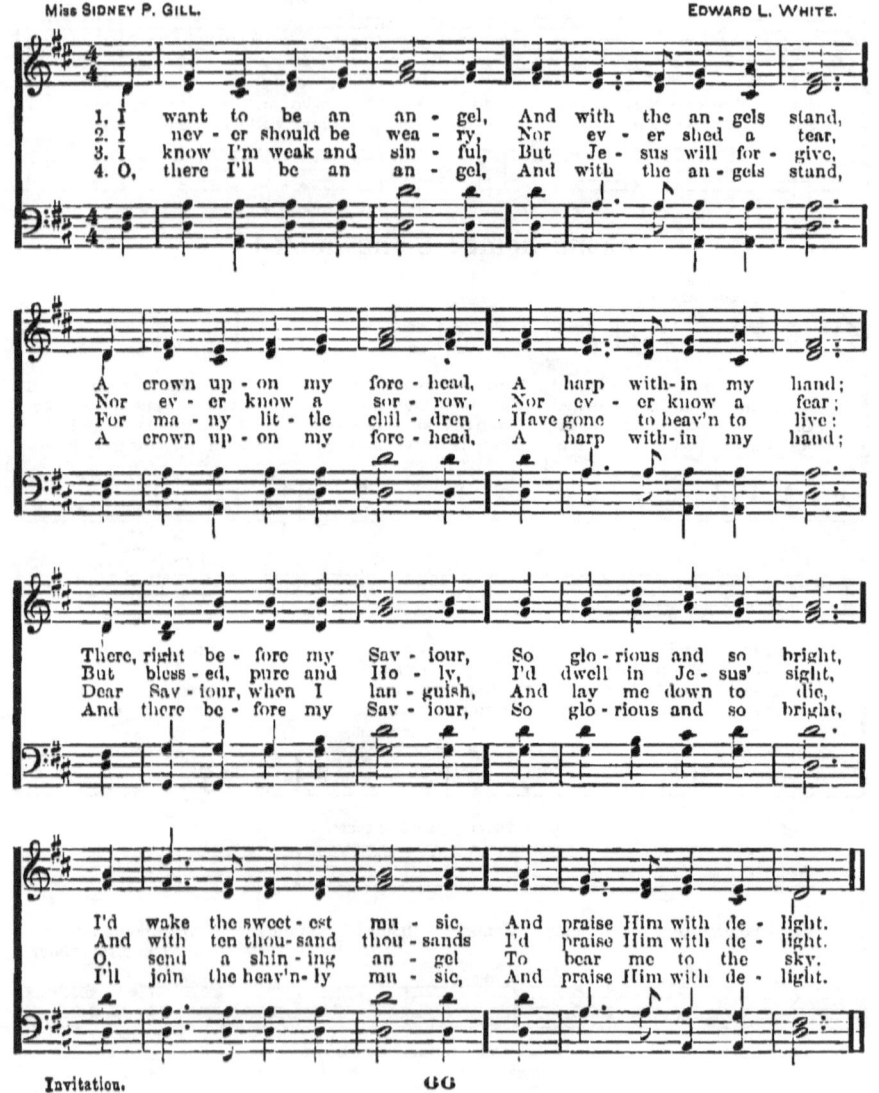

89. Seeking For Me.

A. N.   E. E. HASTY, by per.

1. Je-sus, my Sav-iour, to Beth-le-hem came, Born in a man-ger to sor-row and shame: Oh! it was won-der-ful! blest be His name! Seeking for me, for me, Seek-ing for me, seek-ing for me, Seek-ing for me, seek-ing for me, Oh! it was won-der-ful! blest be His name! Seeking for me, for me.

2. Je-sus, my Sav-iour, on Cal-va-ry's tree, Paid the great debt, and my soul He set free; Oh! it was won-der-ful! how could it be? Dy-ing for me, for me, Dy-ing for me, dy-ing for me, Dy-ing for me, dy-ing for me, Oh! it was won-der-ful! how could it be? Dy-ing for me, for me.

3. Je-sus, my Sav-iour, the same as of old, While I wan-der a-far from the fold, Gen-tly and long He hath plead with my soul, Calling for me, for me, Call-ing for me, call-ing for me, Call-ing for me, call-ing for me, Gen-tly and long He hath plead with my soul, Call-ing for me, for me.

Invitation.

Go, and tell Jesus.—Concluded.

Go, and tell Jesus; Go, and tell Jesus, He on-ly can for-give.

94. Oh, Enter In!

H. BONAR, D. D.
Tenderly.
H. HANKINSON.

1. Strait is the gate, my child; Oh, en-ter in! oh, en-ter in!
2. Strait is the gate, my child; Oh, en-ter in! oh, en-ter in!
3. Strait is the gate, my child; Oh, en-ter in! oh, en-ter in!
4. Strait is the gate, my child; Oh, en-ter in! oh, en-ter in!

And nar-row is the way That leads to heav-'nly day; No more no more de-lay; Oh, en-ter in!
Yet not too strait for thee; 'Tis o-pen, near, and free, God's gate of lib-er-ty; Oh, en-ter in!
It is the gate of love, It leads to rest a-bove, Where sits the ho-ly Dove, Oh, en-ter in!
It is the gate of peace, The door of hope and bliss, Of life and ho-li-ness; Oh, en-ter in!

5 Strait is the gate, my child;
   Oh, enter in! oh, enter in!
Not many find that gate;
Then linger not, nor wait,
It may be soon too late:
   Oh, enter in!

6 Strait is the gate, my child;
   Oh, enter in! oh, enter in!
The Father welcomes thee,
The Saviour beckons thee,
The Spirit pleads with thee,
   Oh, enter in!

Invitation.

95. Wonderful Story of Love.

J. M. D. — Rev. J. M. Driver.

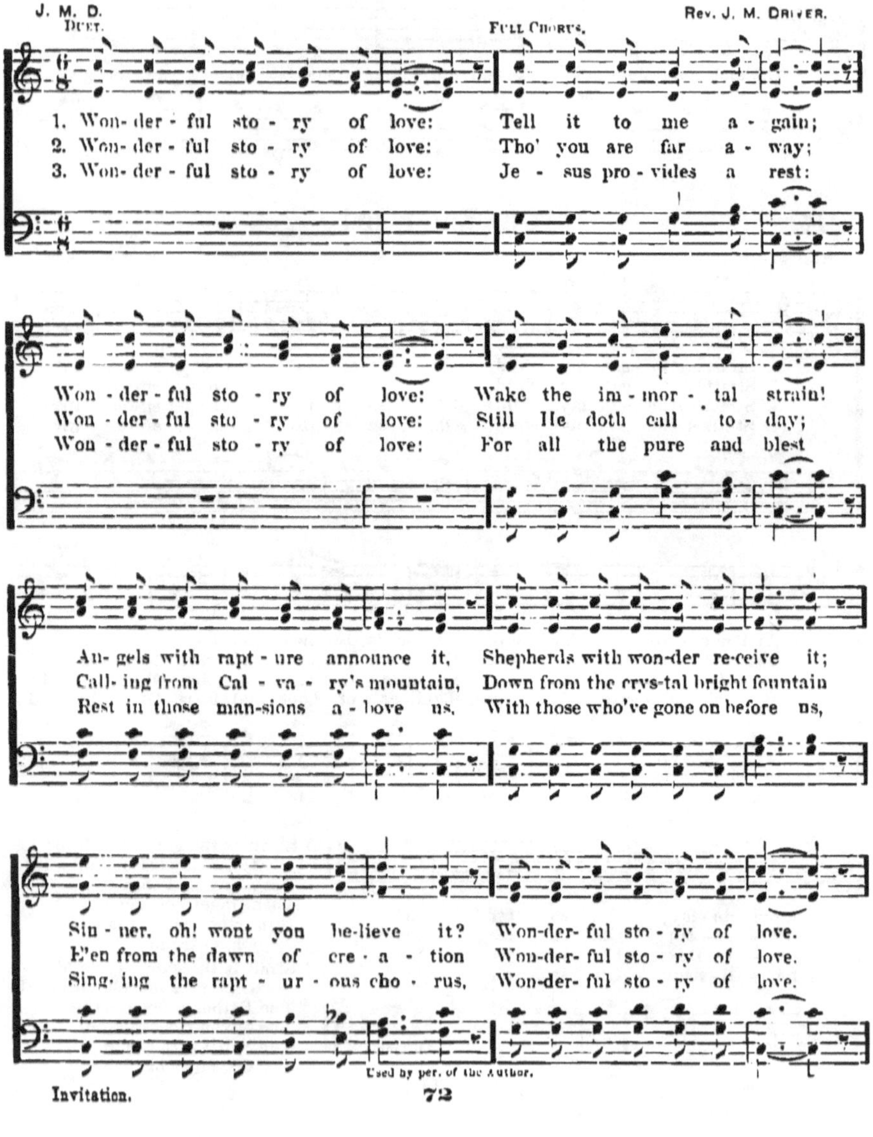

1. Won-der-ful sto-ry of love: Tell it to me a-gain;
2. Won-der-ful sto-ry of love: Tho' you are far a-way;
3. Won-der-ful sto-ry of love: Je-sus pro-vides a rest:

Won-der-ful sto-ry of love: Wake the im-mor-tal strain!
Won-der-ful sto-ry of love: Still He doth call to-day;
Won-der-ful sto-ry of love: For all the pure and blest

An-gels with rapt-ure announce it, Shepherds with won-der re-ceive it;
Call-ing from Cal-va-ry's mountain, Down from the crys-tal bright fountain
Rest in those man-sions a-bove us, With those who've gone on before us,

Sin-ner, oh! wont you be-lieve it? Won-der-ful sto-ry of love.
E'en from the dawn of cre-a-tion Won-der-ful sto-ry of love.
Sing-ing the rapt-ur-ous cho-rus, Won-der-ful sto-ry of love.

Used by per. of the Author.

Invitation.

Wonderful Story of Love.—Concluded.

96. Come, Heavy-Laden One.

W. B. BRADBURY.

1. Come, heavy-la-den one, Sigh-ing for rest; Come, as a wea-ry bird Flies to her nest:
2. Come like the prod-i-gal: He will receive, He will for-give thee all; On-ly be-lieve.
3. Linger not, linger not; Haste while 'tis day: Come, ere the shades of night Close on Thy way.

D.C.—Hark: 'tis Thy Saviour's voice, Calling to Thee, "Come, heavy-la-den one, Come un-to Me."

"Now" the accepted time, "Now" is the day; Come to the mercy-seat—Why wilt Thou stay?
Joy to the mourning heart He will restore; Turn from the path of sin, Wander no more.
Life is a fleeting dream; Soon 'twill be o'er: Turn from its fading joys, Wander no more.

Used by permission

Invitation.

97. Come, Come to Jesus!

Rev. Geo. B. Peck. — Hubert P. Main.
tenderly.

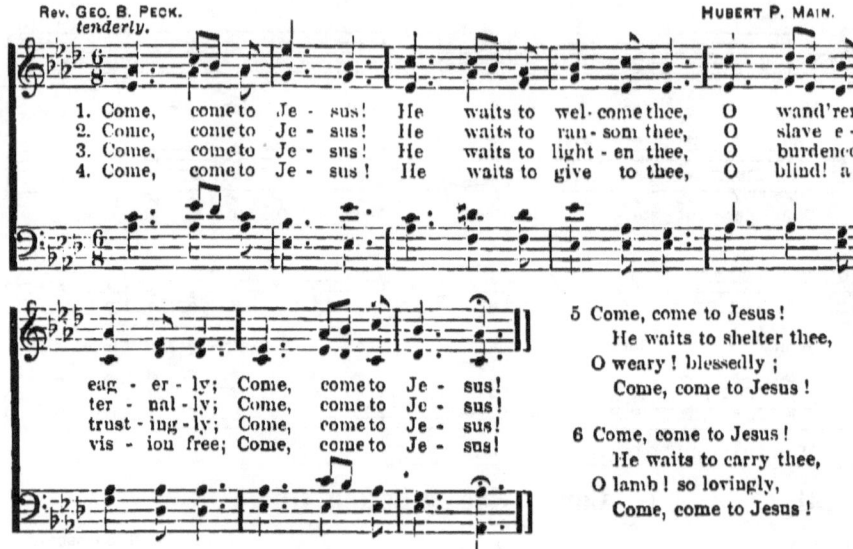

1. Come, come to Jesus! He waits to welcome thee, O wand'rer, eagerly; Come, come to Jesus!
2. Come, come to Jesus! He waits to ransom thee, O slave eternally; Come, come to Jesus!
3. Come, come to Jesus! He waits to lighten thee, O burdened! trustingly; Come, come to Jesus!
4. Come, come to Jesus! He waits to give to thee, O blind! a vision free; Come, come to Jesus!

5 Come, come to Jesus!
   He waits to shelter thee,
O weary! blessedly ;
   Come, come to Jesus!

6 Come, come to Jesus!
   He waits to carry thee,
O lamb! so lovingly,
   Come, come to Jesus!

Used by permission.

98. In the Silent Midnight Watches.

H. B. Stowe. — Rev. H. W. Baker.

1. In the silent midnight watches, List—thy bosom's door, How it knocketh, knocketh, knocketh Evermore!
2. Say not 'tis thy pulse's beating, 'Tis thy heart of sin; 'Tis thy Saviour knocks, and crieth, "Let Me in!"

3 Oh, before you need to call on
   Christ to let you in,
At the gate of heaven wailing
   For thy sin :

4 Hear Him knocking at thy heart,
   Open now the door ;
Bid the loving Saviour enter,
   Evermore.

Invitation.

99. O Have you not Heard.

J. MONTGOMERY.
J. C. ENGELBRECHT. a t.

1. O have you not heard of a beau-ti-ful stream That flows thro' our Father's land?
2. Its fountains are deep, and its wa-ters are pure, And sweet to the wea-ry soul;
3. This beau-ti-ful stream in the Riv-er of Life, It flows for all na-tions free:
4. O will you not drink of that beautiful stream, And dwell on its peaceful shore?

Its wa-ters gleam bright in the heaven-ly light, And rip-ple o'er gold-en sand.
It flows from the throne of Je-ho-vah a-lone, Oh, come where the bright waves roll!
A balm for each wound in its wa-ters is found, Oh, sin-ner, it flows for thee!
The Spir-it says "Come, all ye wea-ry ones, home, And wan-der in sin no more!"

CHORUS.

O, seek that beau-ti-ful stream, Oh, come to that beau-ti-ful stream:
Its wa-ters so free are flow-ing for thee; Come now to that beau-ti-ful stream.

Invitation.

There is a Better World.—Concluded.

harps of gold, and man-sions fair, Oh, so bright, oh, so bright!
in that land of pleas-ure reign: Je - sus died; Je - sus died.
the re-deem'd in glo - ry meet; Come a - way, come a - way.

101.

1 By faith I view my Saviour dying,
   On the tree, on the tree;
   To every nation He is crying,
   "Look to me, look to me!"
   He bids the guilty now draw near,
   Repent, believe, dismiss their fear.
   Hark! hark! what precious words I hear!
   "Mercy's free! mercy free!"

2 Did Christ, when I was sin pursuing,
   Pity me, pity me?
   And did He snatch my soul from ruin?
   Can it be? can it be?
   Oh, yes! He did salvation bring,
   He is my Prophet, Priest, and King:
   And now my happy soul can sing,
   "Mercy's free! mercy's free!"

3 Jesus my weary soul refreshes:
   Mercy's free! mercy's free!
   And every moment Christ is precious
   Unto me, unto me:
   None can describe the bliss I prove,
   While through the wilderness I move:
   All may enjoy the Saviour's love;
   Mercy's free! mercy's free!

4 Long as I live, I'll still be crying,
   "Mercy's free! mercy's free!
   And this shall be my theme when dying,
   "Mercy's free! mercy's free!"
   And when the vale of death I've passed,
   When lodged above the stormy blast,
   I'll sing while endless ages last,
   "Mercy's free! mercy's free!"
   Richard Jukes.

102. Loving Invitation.

J. COURTNAY.

1. { Lo, a lov - ing Friend is wait - ing, He is call - ing thee; (Omit. . . .)
   { Lis - ten to His voice so ten - der, (Omit. . . . . . .) "Come to me."

2 "On the cross for Thee I suffered,
   Death I bore for Thee;
   Canst Thou still refuse My mercy?
   Trust in Me."

3 "Long hast thou been Satan's captive,
   I will set thee free;
   Then, rejoicing in thy freedom,
   Follow Me."

4 Many times has Jesus spoken,
   Now He speaks again;
   Shall thy Saviour's invitation
   Be in vain?

5 Soon that voice will cease its calling,
   Wilt thou still delay?
   Wait no longer; sin grows stronger,
   Yield to-day.

Invitation.

Let the Good Angels Come In.—Concluded.

Invitation.

105. Lord, in this Thy Mercy's Day.

ISAAC WILLIAMS.   A. S. SULLIVAN.

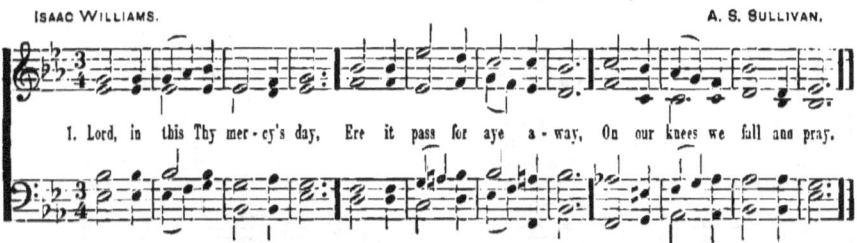

1. Lord, in this Thy mer-cy's day, Ere it pass for aye a-way, On our knees we fall and pray.

2 Holy Jesus, grant us tears,
Fill us with heart-searching fears,
Ere that day of doom appears.

3 Lord, on us Thy Spirit pour,
Kneeling lowly at the door,
Ere it close for evermore.

4 By Thy tears of bitter woe,
For Jerusalem below,
Let us not Thy love forego.

5 Judge and Saviour of our race,
Grant us, when we see Thy face,
With Thy ransomed ones a place.

106.

1 Weeping as they go their way,
Their dear Lord in earth to lay,
Late at even—who are they?

2 These are they who watched to see
Where He hung in agony,
Dying on the accursed tree.

3 All is over—in the tomb
Sleeps He, 'mid its silent gloom,
Till the dawn of Easter come.

4 All is over—fought the fight;
Heaviness is for a night,
Joy comes with the morning light.

5 Leave we in the grave with Him
Sins that shame and doubts that dim,
If our souls would rise with Him.

6 Glory to the Lord who gave,
His pure Body to the grave,
Us from sin and death to save.

W. S. Raymond

107. Heal me, O my Saviour, Heal.

GODFREY THRING.   W. H. MONK.

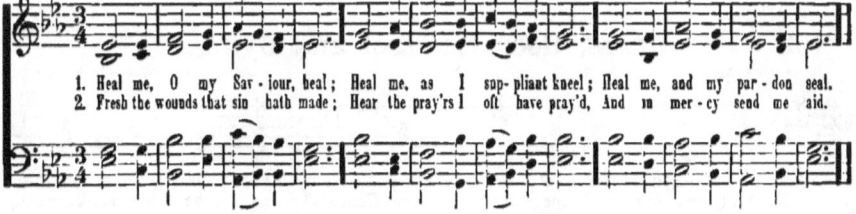

1. Heal me, O my Sav-iour, heal; Heal me, as I sup-pliant kneel; Heal me, and my par-don seal.
2. Fresh the wounds that sin hath made; Hear the pray'rs I oft have pray'd, And in mer-cy send me aid.

3 Thou the true Physician art;
Thou, O Christ, canst health impart,
Binding up the bleeding heart.

4 Other comforters are gone;
Thou canst heal, and Thou alone,
Thou for all my sin atone.

Penitence.

Jesus, Heed Me, Lost and Dying.—Concluded.

Hear, oh, hear, my heart's sore cry-ing; Heed me, or I die!
Come to Thee for help and heal-ing, Heal me, or I die!

3 Not my tears of deep contrition,
Can secure one sin's remission,
Helpless, hopeless my condition:
  Help me, or I die!

4 By Thy cross, where hope is beaming,
By its crimson fountain streaming,
Flowing for the world's redeeming:
  Cleanse me, or I die!

5 So my soul shall praise Thee ever,
For the love which changes never,
From which not e'en death can sever·
  Saved no more to die.

110.

1. Sinner, to the Saviour clinging,
Trembling, trusting, hoping, singing,
Hark! again His voice is ringing:
  Come, O come to Me.

2 Tarry not to count thy treasure;
He will deal it without measure
As thou doest His good pleasure—
  Come, O come to Me.

3 Art thou faint? He stands beside thee;
He shall help thee, guard thee, guide thee:
In His shadow He shall hide thee—
  Come, O come to Me.

Theo. Monod.

111. Weary of Earth.

SAMUEL J. STONE.　　　　　　　　　　J. LANGRAN.

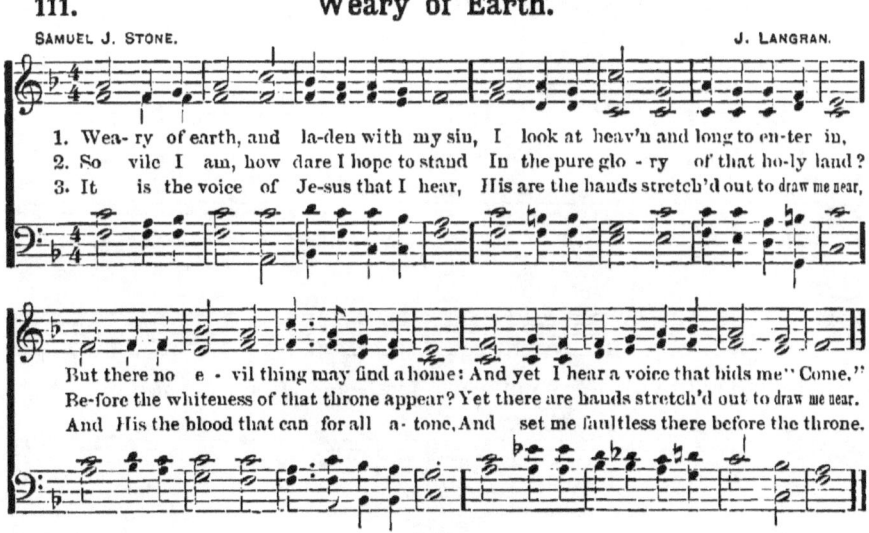

1. Wea-ry of earth, and la-den with my sin, I look at heav'n and long to en-ter in,
2. So vile I am, how dare I hope to stand In the pure glo-ry of that ho-ly land?
3. It is the voice of Je-sus that I hear, His are the hands stretch'd out to draw me near,

But there no e-vil thing may find a home: And yet I hear a voice that bids me "Come."
Be-fore the whiteness of that throne appear? Yet there are hands stretch'd out to draw me near.
And His the blood that can for all a-tone, And set me faultless there before the throne.

Penitence.

112. To Jesus I will Go.

FANNY J. CROSBY.   W. H. DOANE.

1. There's a gen-tle voice within calls a-way, 'Tis a warning I have heard o'er and o'er;
2. He has promised all my sins to for-give, If I ask in sim-ple faith for His love;
3. I will try to bear the cross in my youth, And be faithful to its cause till I die;
4. Still the gen-tle voice within calls a-way, And its warning I have heard o'er and o'er;

But my heart is melt-ed now, I o-bey; From my Saviour I will wan-der no more.
In His ho-ly word I learn how to live, And to la-bor for His king-dom a-bove.
If with cheerful step I walk in the truth, I shall wear a star-ry crown by and by.
But my heart is melt-ed now, I o-bey; From my Saviour I will wan-der no more.

CHORUS.

Yes, I will go; yes I will go; To Je-sus I will go and be saved;

Yes, I will go; yes I will go; To Je-sus I will go and be saved.

Copyright, 1869, in "Bright Jewels," by Biglow & Main.

Penitence.

115. O Eyes that are Weary.

Anon.   From DONIZETTI.

1. O eyes that are weary, and hearts that are sore, Look up un-to Je-sus, now sor-row no more! The light of His countenance shineth so bright, That here, as in heav-en, there need be no night.
2. While looking to Je-sus, my heart can-not fear; I trem-ble no more when I see Je-sus near; I know that His presence my safeguard will be, For, "Why are ye troubled?" He saith un-to me.

3 Still looking to Jesus, O may I be found,
When Jordan's dark waters encompass me round;
They bear me away in His presence to be;
I see Him still nearer whom always I see.

116. Resting in Thy Love.

Rev. R. W. Todd.   HARRY SANDERS.

1. While way-worn and wea-ry, I jour-ney a-long, Dear Sav-iour, Thy love is the theme of my song; Thy smile is my bea-con, as onward I move; Thy cross is my shel-ter—I rest in Thy love.
2. While bur-den'd with sor-row, and la-dened with woe, Dear Sav-iour, to Thee 'neath Thy cross will I go; I think of Thy sor-row and anguish for me, And yield at Thy bid-ding, my sor-rows to Thee.

3 And when—all the pangs of mortality o'er—
I join with the blood-washed who sing on the shore;
I'll dwell with the pure in Thy temple above;
For ever and ever I'll rest in Thy love.

Used by arr. with Oliver Ditson Co., owners of Copyright.

Faith.

117. I Love to Hear the Story.

Emily H. Miller — French Air.

1. I love to hear the story Which angels' voices tell,
   How once the King of glory Came down on Earth to dwell.
   I am both weak and sinful; But this I surely know,
   The Lord came down to save me; Because He loved me so!

2. I'm glad my bless-èd Saviour Was once a child like me,
   To show how pure and holy His little ones might be;
   And if I try to follow His footsteps here below,
   He never will forsake me; Because He loves me so!

3. To sing His love and mercy My sweetest songs I'll raise,
   And tho' I cannot see Him I know He hears my praise;
   For He has kindly promised That even I may go
   To sing among His angels; Because He loves me so!

Ref.—I love to hear the story Which angels' voices tell,
How once the King of glory Came down on Earth to dwell.

Faith.

118.

1 To-day Thy mercy calls me
   To wash away my sin.
 However great my trespass,
   Whate'er I may have been,
 However long from mercy
   I may have turned away,
 Thy blood, O Christ, can cleanse me,
   And make me white to-day.

REF.—To-day Thy gate is open
   And all who enter in,
 Shall find a Father's welcome,
   And pardon for their sin.

2 To-day the Father calls me,
   The Holy Spirit waits,
 The blessèd angels gather
   Around the heavenly gates,
 The past shall be forgotten,
   A present joy be given,
 A future grace be promised,
   A glorious crown in heaven.
                  Oswald Allen.

119.

1 The Homeland! O the Homeland!
   The land of souls freeborn!
 No gloomy night is known there,
   But aye the fadeless morn:
 My Lord is in the Homeland,
   With angels bright and fair;
 No sinful thing nor evil,
   Can ever enter there.

REF.—The Homeland! O the Homeland!
   The land of souls freeborn!
 No gloomy night is known there,
   But aye the fadeless morn.

2 For loved ones in the Homeland
   Are waiting me to come
 Where neither death nor sorrow
   Invade their holy home:
 O dear, dear native Country!
   O rest and peace above!
 Christ bring us all to the Homeland
   Of His eternal love.
                  Hugh R. Haweis.

120. We may not Climb the Heavenly Steeps.

J. G. WHITTIER.   W. V. WALLACE.

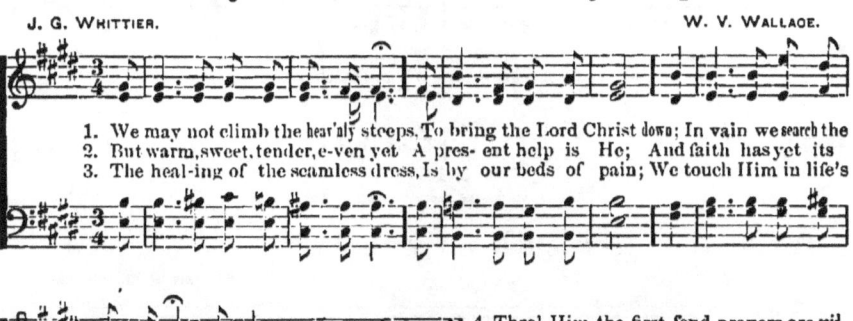

1. We may not climb the heav'nly steeps, To bring the Lord Christ down; In vain we search the
2. But warm, sweet, tender, e-ven yet A pres-ent help is He; And faith has yet its
3. The heal-ing of the seamless dress, Is by our beds of pain; We touch Him in life's

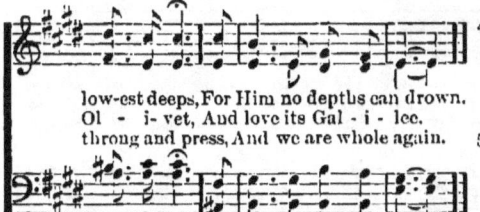

low-est deeps, For Him no depths can drown.
Ol - i - vet, And love its Gal - i - lee.
throng and press, And we are whole again.

4 Thro' Him the first fond prayers are said,
   Our lips of childhood frame;
 The last low whispers of our dead
   Are burdened with His name.

5 O Lord and Master of us all,
   Whate'er our name or sign,
 We own Thy sway, we hear Thy call,
   We test our lives by Thine!

Used by arr. with Oliver Ditson Co., owners of Copyright.

Faith.

I left it all with Jesus.—Concluded.

When by faith I saw Him on the tree, Heard Him gently whisper, "Tis for thee,"
Now to gild the tear-drop with His smile, Make the desert garden bloom awhile;
Hope has dropp'd her anchor, found her rest, In the calm sure haven of His breast.

From my heart the burden roll'd away! Happy day! From my heart the burden roll'd away! Happy day!
When my weakness leaneth on His might, All seems light; When my weakness leaneth on His might, All seems light.
Love esteems it heaven to abide At His side, Love esteems it heaven to abide At His side.

123. A Brother's Care.

HORATIUS BONAR, D.D.   Mrs. CHARLES BARNARD.

1. Yes! for me, for me He careth, With a brother's tender care, Yes! with me, with me He shareth,
2. Yes! o'er me, o'er me He watcheth, Ceaseless watcheth night and day; Yes! e'en me, e'en me He snatcheth
3. Yes! for me He standeth pleading At the mercy-seat above; Ever for me interceding,

Ev-'ry burden, ev-'ry care.
From the perils of the way.
Constant in untiring love.

4 Yes! in me, in me He dwelleth,
  I in Him, and He in me;
And my empty soul He filleth,
  Here, and through eternity.

5 Thus I wait for His returning,
  Singing all the way to heaven;
Such the joyful song of morning,
  Such the joyful song of even.

Faith

125. Tell me ye Wingèd Winds.

CHAS. MACKAY.   Fr. MENDELSSOHN.

1. Tell me, ye wingèd winds, That round my pathway roar; Do ye not know some spot Where mortals weep no more? Some lone and pleasant dell, Some valley in the west, Where, free from toil and pain, The weary soul may rest? The loud winds dwindled to a whisper low, And sigh'd for pity as they answer'd, "no!"

2. Tell me, ye mighty deep, Whose billows round me play; Know'st thou some favor'd spot, Some island far away, Where weary man may find The bliss for which he sighs; Where sorrow never lives, And friendship never dies? The loud waves roaring in perpetual flow, Stopp'd for a while and sigh'd to answer, "no!"

3. Tell me, my sacred soul, O tell me, Hope and Faith, Is there no resting-place From sorrow, sin and death? Is there no happy spot Where mortals may be blest,— Where grief may find a balm, And weariness, a rest? Faith, Hope and Love, best boons to mortals giv'n, Wav'd their bright wings, and whisper'd, "yes, in heav'n!"

Faith.

'Tis Sweet to Know—Concluded.

near, ... And sweeter still .... that He will hear......
that He is near, And sweeter still that He will hear.

127. Shine Out, Oh Life Divine.

J. G. WHITTIER   Rev. T. R. MATTHEWS.

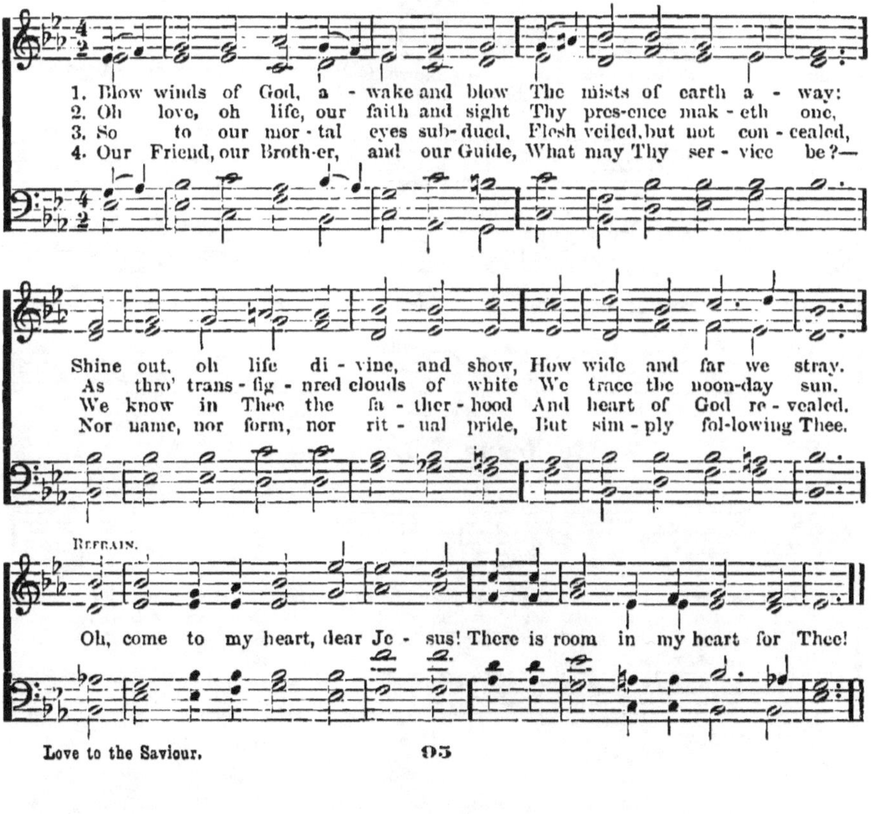

1. Blow winds of God, a-wake and blow The mists of earth a-way:
2. Oh love, oh life, our faith and sight Thy pres-ence mak-eth one,
3. So to our mor-tal eyes sub-dued, Flesh veiled, but not con-cealed,
4. Our Friend, our Broth-er, and our Guide, What may Thy ser-vice be?—

Shine out, oh life di-vine, and show, How wide and far we stray.
As thro' trans-fig-ured clouds of white We trace the noon-day sun.
We know in Thee the fa-ther-hood And heart of God re-vealed.
Nor name, nor form, nor rit-ual pride, But sim-ply fol-lowing Thee.

REFRAIN.
Oh, come to my heart, dear Je-sus! There is room in my heart for Thee!

Love to the Saviour.

My Jesus, I Love Thee.—Concluded.

My gra-cious Re-deem-er, my Sav-iour art Thou; If ev-er I loved Thee, my Je-sus, 'tis now.
I love Thee for wear-ing the thorns on Thy brow; If ev-er I loved Thee, my Je-sus, 'tis now.
I'll sing with the glit-ter-ing crown on my brow; If ev-er I loved Thee, my Je-sus, 'tis now.

130. The Name of Jesus.

Rev. W. O. Cushing.   Hubert P. Main.

1. O the name, the name of Je-sus, How my heart it thrills! Sweet-est mu-sic floating
2. Breathe, O breathe the name of Je-sus, Low be-fore the throne; Own-ing all your sin and
3. When thy heart is sad and lone-ly, Sin-ful tho' it be, Thou canst plead the name of

REFRAIN.

round me, And my soul it fills.
weak-ness, Trust-ing Him a - lone.
Je - sus, Je - sus died for thee.

O e precious name of Je - sus,
Breath it low in pray'r; At the cross of Je-sus bend-ing, God will hear thee there.

Copyright, 1880, by Biglow & Main.

Love to the Saviour.

A little Talk with Jesus.—Concluded.

There is nothing that giv-eth me com-fort Like a lit-tle talk with Him.

132. Keep Thou my Way, O Lord.

FANNY J. CROSBY.   HUBERT P. MAIN.

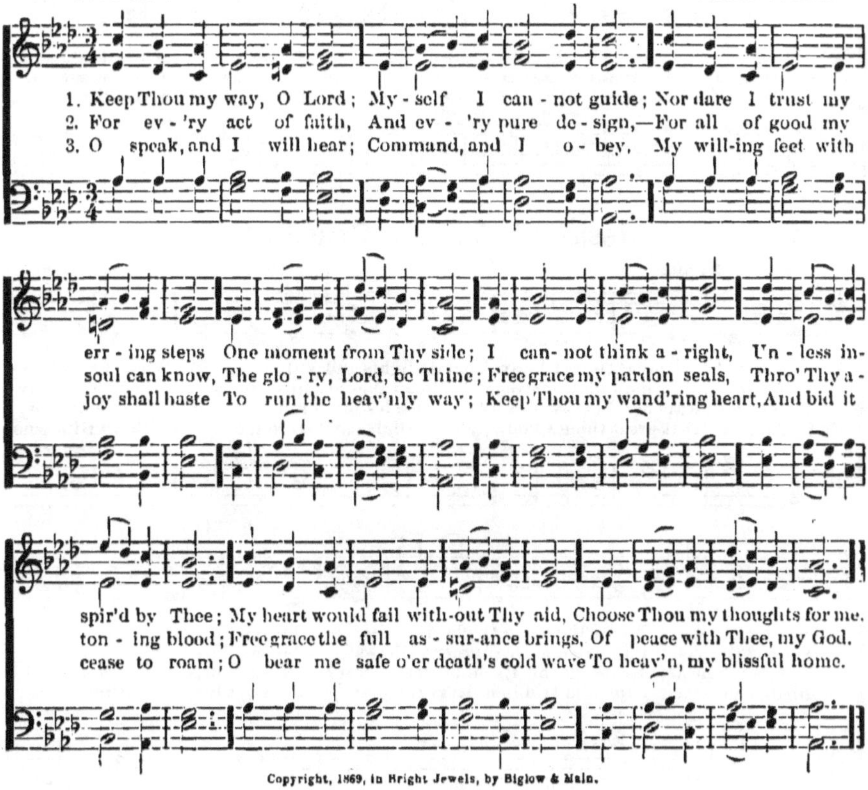

1. Keep Thou my way, O Lord; My-self I can-not guide; Nor dare I trust my err-ing steps One moment from Thy side; I can-not think a-right, Un-less in-spir'd by Thee; My heart would fail with-out Thy aid, Choose Thou my thoughts for me.
2. For ev-'ry act of faith, And ev-'ry pure de-sign,—For all of good my soul can know, The glo-ry, Lord, be Thine; Free grace my pardon seals, Thro' Thy a-ton-ing blood; Free grace the full as-sur-ance brings, Of peace with Thee, my God.
3. O speak, and I will hear; Command, and I o-bey, My will-ing feet with joy shall haste To run the heav'nly way; Keep Thou my wand'ring heart, And bid it cease to roam; O bear me safe o'er death's cold wave To heav'n, my blissful home.

Copyright, 1869, in Bright Jewels, by Biglow & Main.

Love to the Saviour.

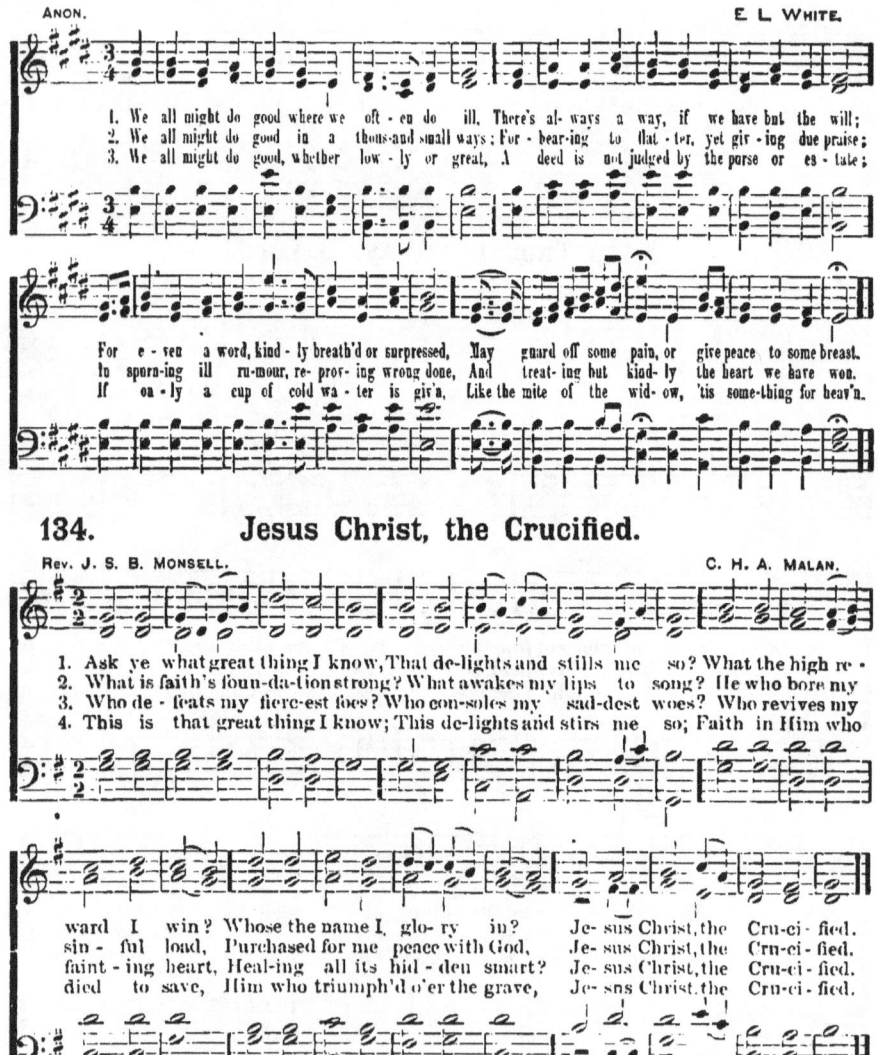

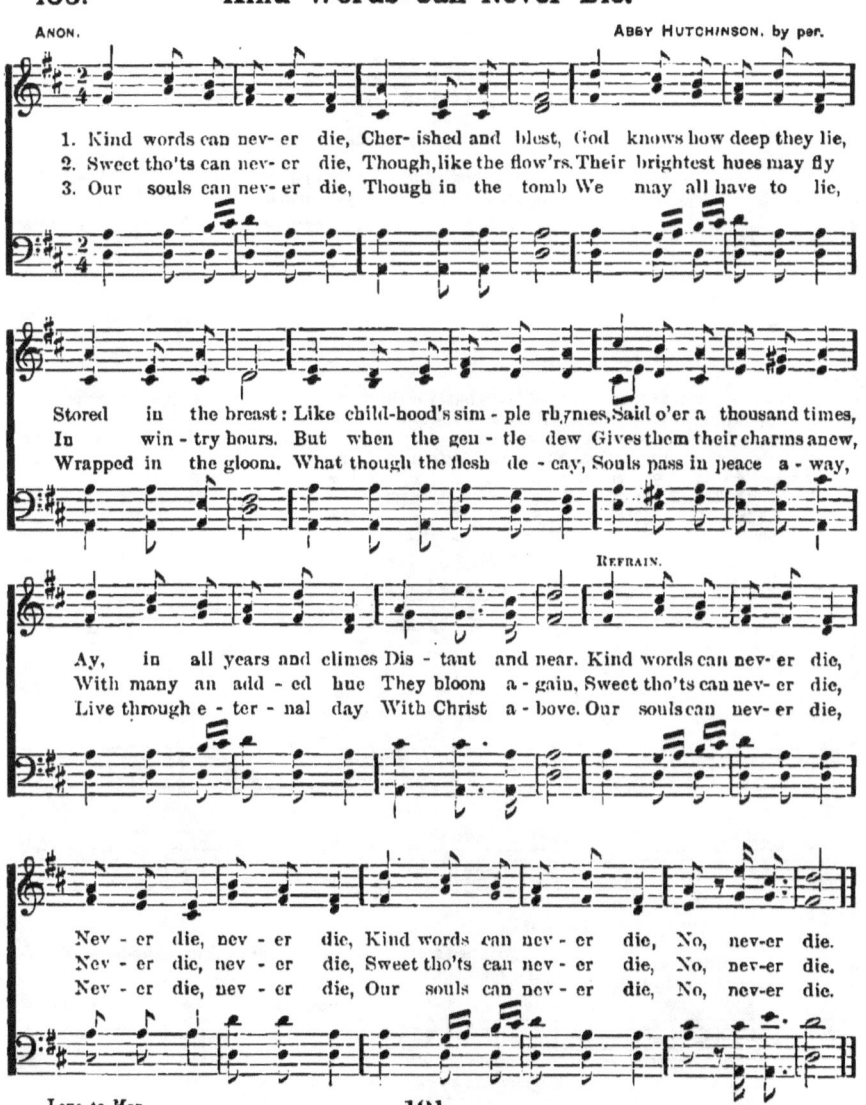

Scatter Seeds of Kindness.—Concluded.

kind-ness,   Then scat-ter seeds of kind-ness, For our reaping by and by.

137. Lord, what Offering shall we Bring.

JOHN TAYLOR.   W. A. MOZART.

1. Lord, what offering shall we bring, At Thine al-tars when we bow? Hearts, the pure, un-
2. Will-ing hands to lead the blind, Blind and wounded, feed the poor; Love, em-brac-ing

sullied spring Whence the kind affections flow; Soft compassion's feel-ing soul, By the
all our kind, Char-i-ty, with lib-eral store: Teach us, O Thou heav-enly King, Thus to

melt-ing eye expressed! Sympathy, at whose control, Sorrow leaves the wounded breast.
show our grate-ful mind; Thus th' accepted offering bring, Love to Thee and all mankind.

Love to Man.

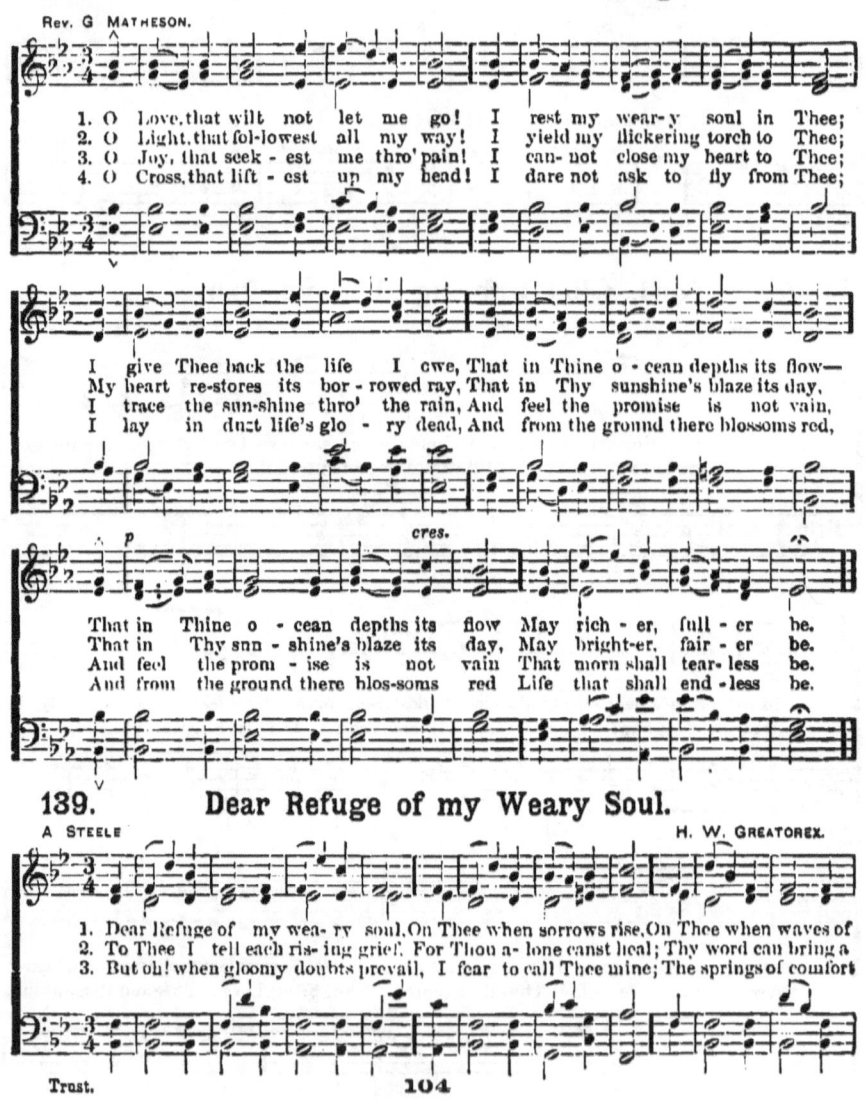

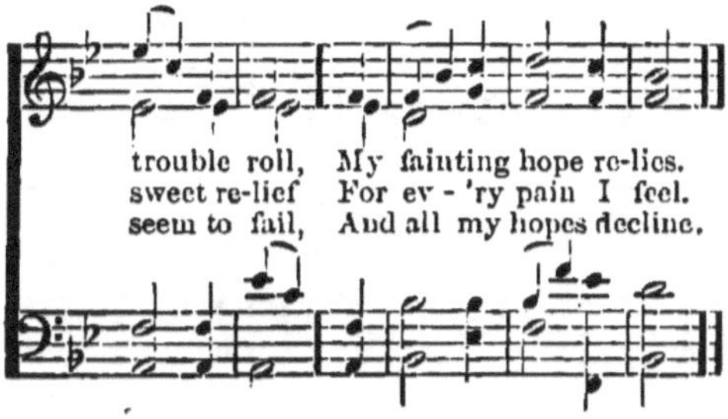

Dear Refuge of my Weary Soul.—Concluded.

trouble roll, My fainting hope re-lies.
sweet re-lief For ev-'ry pain I feel.
seem to fail, And all my hopes decline.

4 Yet, gracious God, where shall I flee?
Thou art my only trust;
And still my soul would cleave to Thee,
Though prostrate in the dust.

5 Thy mercy-seat is open still,
Here let my soul retreat,
With humble hope attend Thy will,
And wait beneath Thy feet.

140. O Lord My Heart is Thine.

FANNY J. CROSBY.   HUBERT P. MAIN.

1. O Lord my heart is Thine, Thy love a-bides in me; My faith is anchored
2. O Lord my heart is Thine, And Thou Thy trust wilt keep; Thy voice will calm its
3. O Lord my heart is Thine, And with my soul 'tis well; By cool-ing streams Thou
4. O Lord my heart is Thine, And when its chords shall break, 'Twill soar a-loft on

on Thy word, My life is hid with Thee.
troubled waves, And lull its cares to sleep.
leadest me, And there in peace I dwell.
ea-gle wings, A sweet-er song to make.

REFRAIN.

No harm shall e'er be-tide me, For Thou Thy-self wilt guide me, And Thou, O Lord, wilt safely hide me, My heart is Thine.

Copyright 1886, by Biglow & Main.

Trust.

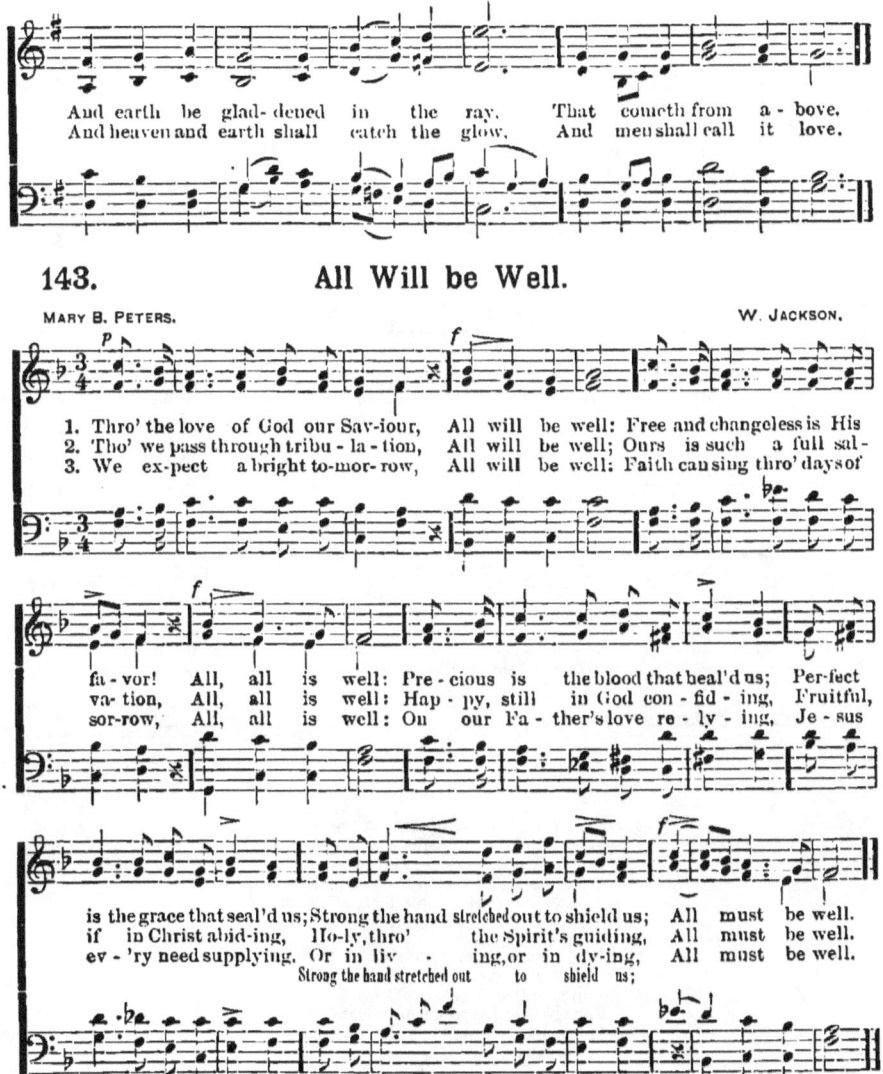

144. If I Could only Know!

Anon
THOS HASTINGS

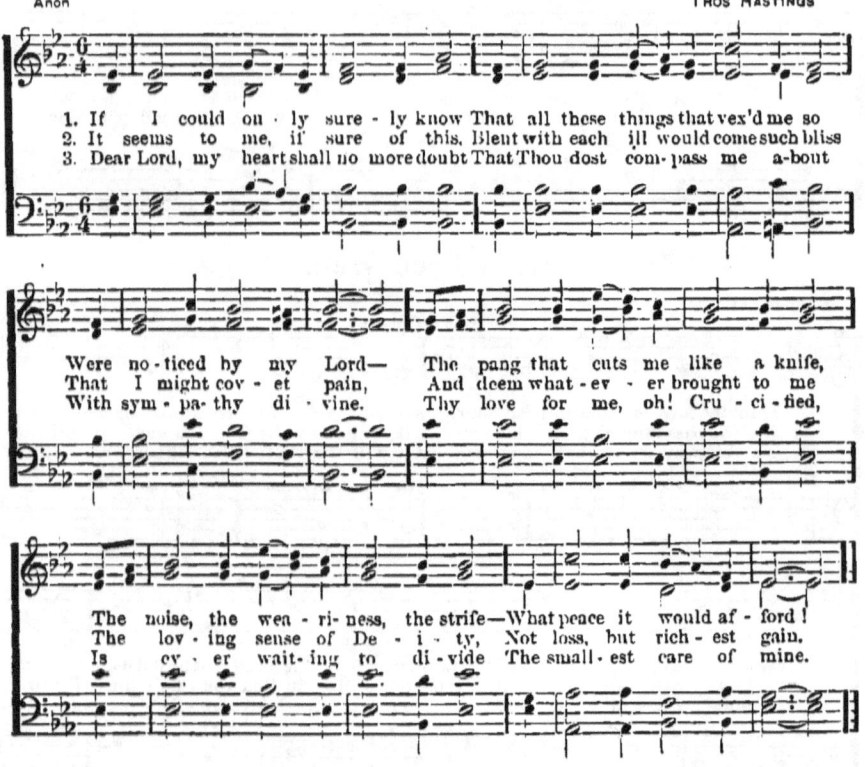

1. If I could only surely know That all these things that vex'd me so
   Were noticed by my Lord—
   The pang that cuts me like a knife,
   The noise, the weariness, the strife—What peace it would afford!

2. It seems to me, if sure of this, Blent with each ill would come such bliss
   That I might covet pain,
   And deem whatever brought to me
   The loving sense of Deity, Not loss, but richest gain.

3. Dear Lord, my heart shall no more doubt That Thou dost compass me about
   With sympathy divine.
   Thy love for me, oh! Crucified,
   Is ever waiting to divide The smallest care of mine.

145.

1 Fear not, O little flock, the foe
   Who madly seeks your overthrow;
   Dread not His rage and power;
   What though your courage sometimes faints,
   His seeming triumph o'er God's saints
   Lasts but a little hour.

2 Be of good cheer; your cause belongs
   To Him who can avenge your wrongs;
   Leave it to Him, our Lord!
   Though hidden yet from mortal eyes,
   He sees the hosts that shall arise
   To save us by His word.

Tr. by C. Winkworth.

Trust.

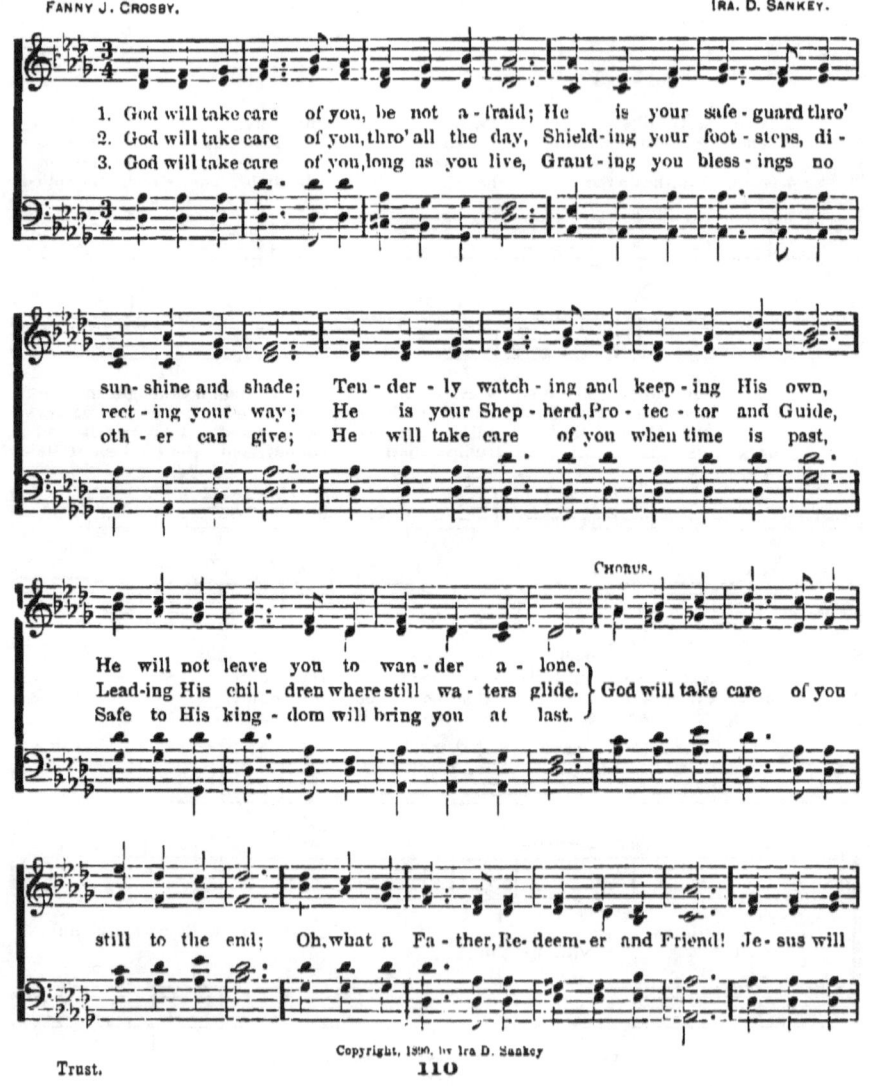

God will take Care of You.—Concluded.

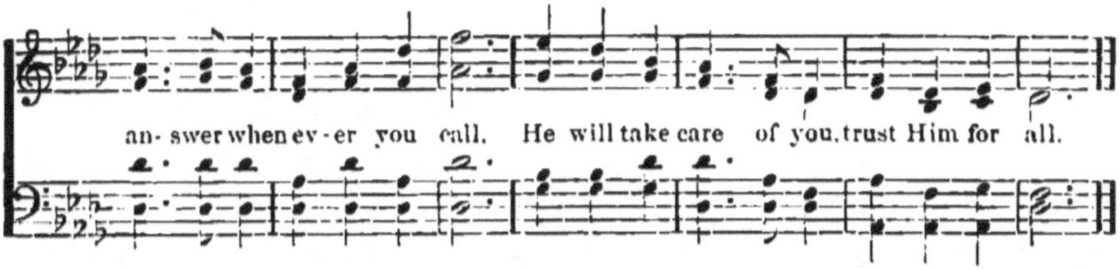

an-swer when ev-er you call. He will take care of you, trust Him for all.

148. The Lord will Provide.

Mrs. M. A. W. Cook.   Philip Phillips, by per.

1. In some way or oth-er the Lord will pro-vide: It may not be *my* way,
2. At some time or oth-er the Lord will pro-vide: It may not be *my* time,
3. De-spond then no long-er: the Lord will pro-vide; And this be the to-ken—
4. March on then right bold-ly; the sea shall di-vide; The path-way made glo-rious,

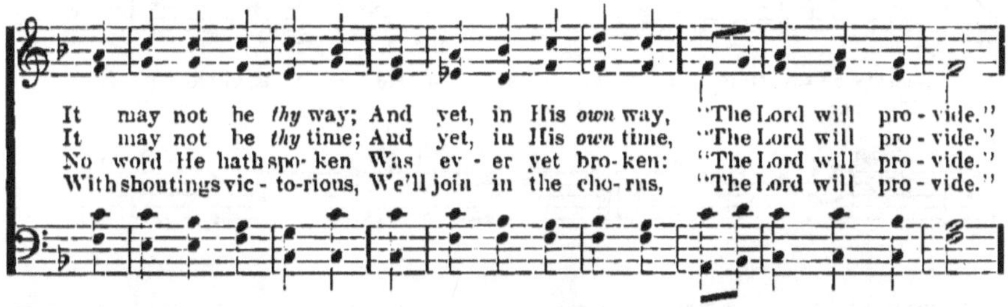

It may not be *thy* way; And yet, in His *own* way, "The Lord will pro-vide."
It may not be *thy* time; And yet, in His *own* time, "The Lord will pro-vide."
No word He hath spo-ken Was ev-er yet bro-ken: "The Lord will pro-vide."
With shoutings vic-to-rious, We'll join in the cho-rus, "The Lord will pro-vide."

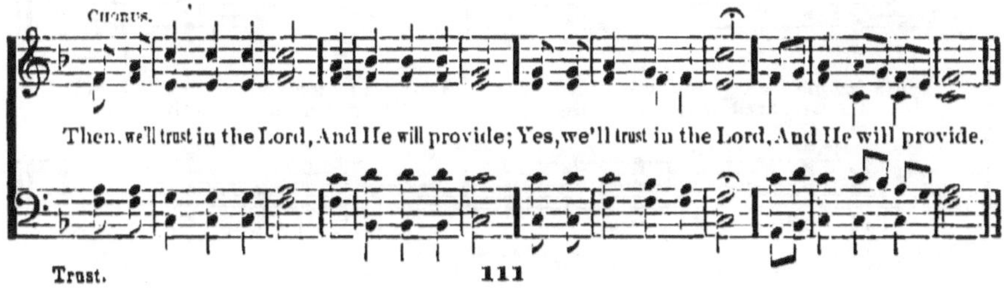

Chorus.

Then, we'll trust in the Lord, And He will provide; Yes, we'll trust in the Lord, And He will provide.

Trust.

150. Sheltered in Thee.

F. M. DAVIS.
FRANK M. DAVIS, by per.

1. I am safe in the Rock that is high-er than I, This my ref-uge thro' storms e'er shall be; Tho' my frail bark is toss'd on the bil-lows' mad foam, Yet I'm shel-ter'd for - ev - er in Thee.
2. I am safe in the Rock that was riv-en for me, From the pow'r of the temp-ter I'm free; Tho' my path-way be dark and the storms sweep the sky, Yet se-cure-ly I'm shel-ter'd in Thee.
3. I am safe in the Rock, let what-ev-er be-tide, Death and hell have no ter-ror to me; I can walk with-out fear thro' the shad-ow-y vale, For se-cure-ly I'm shel-ter'd in Thee.

CHORUS.

Shel-ter'd in Thee, shel-ter'd in Thee, O Thou blest Rock of A - ges, I am shel-ter'd in Thee.

Trust.

151. Forever Blessed.

Rev. W. Walsham How.   Arr. fr. John E. Gould.

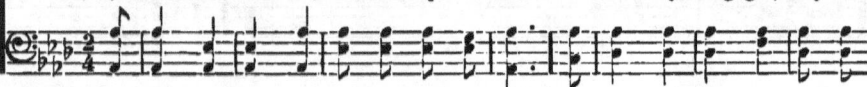

1. For all the saints, who from their la-bors rest, Who Thee by faith be-fore the
2. Thou wast their Rock, their Fortress and their Might; Thou, Lord, their Captain in the
3. O may Thy sol-diers, faith-ful, true, and bold, Fight as the saints, who no-bly
4. Oh, blest com-mun-ion, fel-low-ship di-vine! We fee-bly strug-gle; they in

world con-fess'd, Thy name, O Je-sus, be for-ev-er blessed, For-ev-er blessed.
well-fought fight; Thou, in the darkness drear, their one true Light, Their one true Light.
fought of old, And win with them the victor's crown of gold, Their crown of gold.
glo-ry shine Yet all are one in Thee, for all are Thine, For all are Thine.

5 But lo! there breaks a yet more glorious day;
  The saints triumphant rise in bright array;
  The King of Glory passes on His way!
    Pursues His way!

6 From earth's wide bounds, from ocean's farthest coast,
  Thro' gates of pearl streams in the countless [host,
  Singing to Father, Son, and Holy Ghost,
    "Hallelujah!"

152.

1 Forsake me not! O Thou, my Lord, my Light!
  I lift mine eyes unto Thy holy height,
  And trust Thee with a child's sweet trust untaught:
    Forsake me not!

2 Forsake me not! By sorrow oft depressed,
  On Thee alone, Almighty Power, I rest!
  Strength faileth me; be Thou my strength—Christ-bought:
    Forsake me not!

3 Forsake me not! Help me to know Thy way!
  Let me at last, at closing of my day,
  Into the light of Thy dear face be brought!
    Forsake me not!
                Tr. by Mrs. J. P. Morgan.

153. Crossing the Bar.

ALFRED TENNYSON. Died October 6, 1892.
GEO. F. ROOT.

1. Sun-set and Even-ing Star, And one clear call for me! And may there be no moan-ing bar When I put out to sea.
2. But mov-ing tide a-sleep, Too full for sound and foam, When that which drew from out the deep Turns to its ear-liest home.

3 Twilight and Evening Bell,
And after that the dark!
And may there be no sad farewell,
When I at last embark.

4 For tho' from Time and Place,
The flood may bear me far,
I hope to see my Pilot's face,
When I have crossed the bar.

154. Leaning on Thee.

CHARLOTTE ELLIOTT.
W. HENMAN.

1. Lean-ing on Thee, my Guide, my Friend, My gra-cious Sav-iour! I am blest; Though wea-ry, Thou dost con-de-scend To be my rest.
2. Lean-ing on Thee, with child-like faith, To Thee, with fu-ture I con-fide; Each step of life's un-trod-den path Thy love will guide.
3. Lean-ing on Thee, though faint and weak, Too weak a-noth-er voice to hear, Thy heav-'nly ac-cents com-fort speak, "Be of good cheer."
4. Lean-ing on Thee, no fear a-larms; Calm-ly I stand on death's dark brink; I feel the "ev-er-last-ing arms," I can-not sink.

Trust.

155. Thou art my Hiding-place, O Lord.

THOMAS RAFFLES.
Andante.

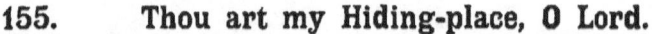

1. Thou art my hid-ing-place, O Lord! On Thee I fix my trust, En-cour-ag'd by Thy ho-ly word, A fee-ble child of dust. I have no ar-gu-ment be-side, I urge no oth-er plea; And 'tis enough the Saviour died, The Saviour died for me.
2. 'Mid tri-als heav-y to be borne, When mortal strength is vain, A heart with grief and an-guish torn, A bod-y rack'd with pain; Ah, what could give the suff'rer rest, Bid ev-'ry murmur flee, But this, the witness in my breast That Je-sus died for me.
3. And when Thine awful voice commands This bod-y to de-cay, And life, in its last ling'ring sands, Is ebbing fast a-way; Then, tho' it be in ac-cents weak, And faint and tremblingly, O give me strength in death to speak, "My Saviour died for me."

156.

1 Father, I know that all my life
  Is portioned out for me;
  The changes that will surely come
  I do not fear to see:
  ‖: I ask Thee for a present mind,
  Intent on pleasing Thee. :‖

2 I would not have the restless will
  That hurries to and fro,
  That seeks for some great thing to do,
  Or secret thing to know:
  ‖: I would be treated as a child,
  And guided where I go. :‖

3 I ask Thee for the daily strength,
  To none that ask denied,
  A mind to blend with outward life,
  While keeping at Thy side;
  ‖: Content to fill a little space,
  If Thou be glorified. :‖

4 And if some things I do not ask,
  Among my blessings be,
  I'd have my spirit filled the more
  With grateful love to Thee;
  ‖: More careful—not to serve Thee much,
  But please Thee perfectly. :‖

Miss A. L. Waring.

Trust.

158. Beneath His Wing.

HORATIUS BONAR, D.D.
Arr. H. P. M.

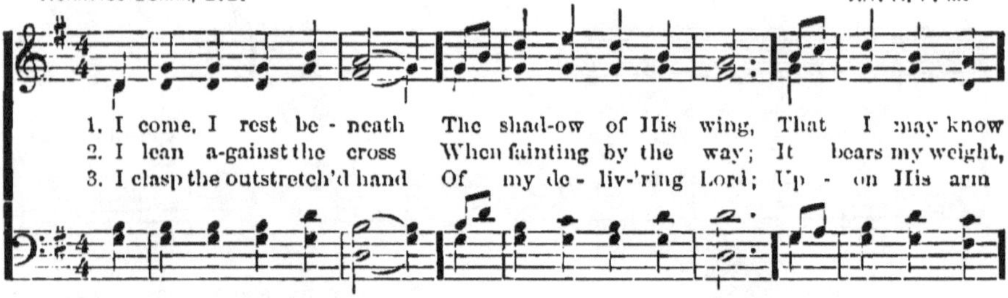

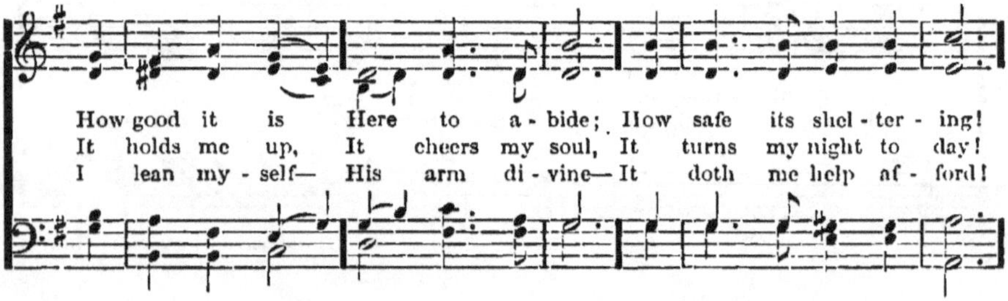

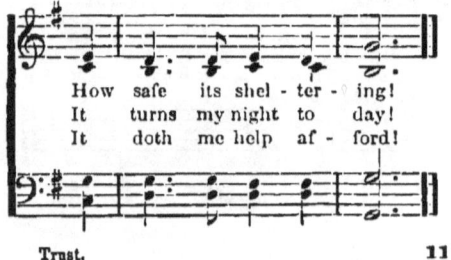

1. I come, I rest beneath The shadow of His wing, That I may know How good it is Here to abide; How safe its sheltering! How safe its sheltering! How good it is Here to abide; How safe its sheltering!
2. I lean against the cross When fainting by the way; It bears my weight, It holds me up, It cheers my soul, It turns my night to day! It turns my night to day! It holds me up, It cheers my soul, It turns my night to day!
3. I clasp the outstretch'd hand Of my deliv'ring Lord; Upon His arm I lean myself— His arm divine— It doth me help afford! It doth me help afford! I lean myself— His arm divine— It doth me help afford!

4 I hear the gracious words
   He speaketh to my soul;
   They whisper rest,
   They banish fear,
   They say, "be strong,"
   They make my spirit whole!

5 I look and live and move;
   I listen to the voice
   Saying to me
   That God is love,
   That God is light:
   I listen, and rejoice!

Trust.

159. As Trustful as a Child.

JAMES D. BURNS.   National Air of Holland.

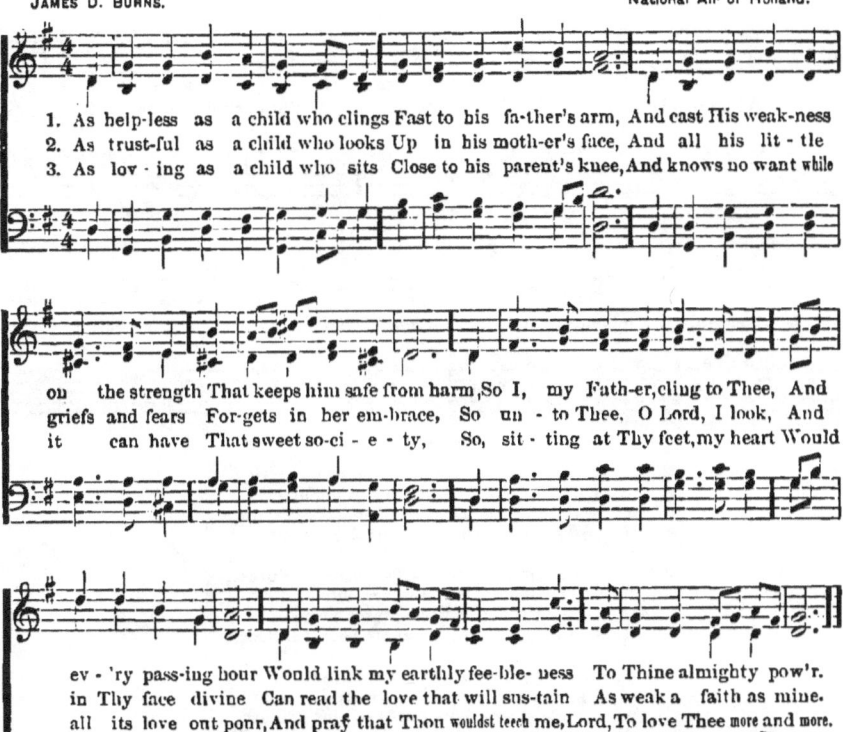

1. As help-less as a child who clings Fast to his fa-ther's arm, And cast His weak-ness on the strength That keeps him safe from harm, So I, my Fath-er, cling to Thee, And ev - 'ry pass-ing hour Would link my earthly fee-ble-ness To Thine almighty pow'r.
2. As trust-ful as a child who looks Up in his moth-er's face, And all his lit - tle griefs and fears For-gets in her em-brace, So un - to Thee, O Lord, I look, And in Thy face divine Can read the love that will sus-tain As weak a faith as mine.
3. As lov - ing as a child who sits Close to his parent's knee, And knows no want while it can have That sweet so-ci - e - ty, So, sit - ting at Thy feet, my heart Would all its love out pour, And pray that Thou wouldst teach me, Lord, To love Thee more and more.

160.

1 O Thou, in all Thy might so far,
   In all Thy love so near;—
Beyond the range of sun and star,
   And yet beside us here:—
What heart can comprehend Thy name,
   Or, searching, find Thee out?
Who art within, a quickening Flame,
   A Presence round about!

2 O sweeter than all else besides,
   The tender mystery
That like a veil of shadow hides
   The light we may not see!
Yet though we know Thee but in part,
   We ask not, Lord, for more:
Enough for us to know Thou art,
   To love Thee and adore!

Hosmer.

Trust.

161. When Winds are Raging.

Mrs. H. B. Stowe. Lowell Mason.

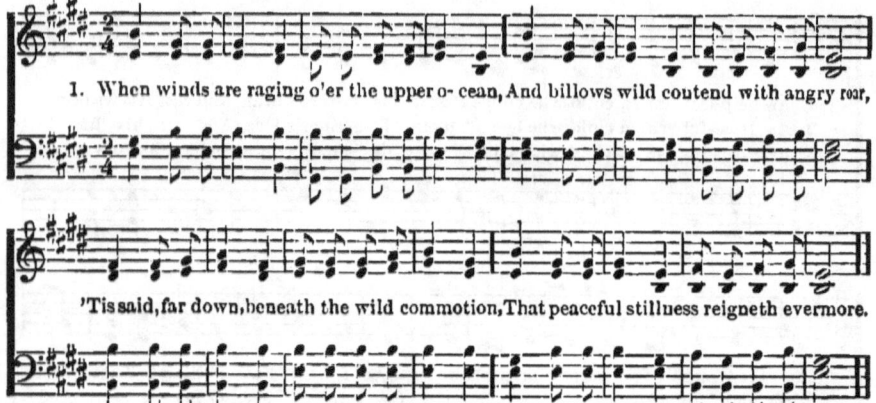

1. When winds are raging o'er the upper o-cean, And billows wild contend with angry roar,
'Tis said, far down, beneath the wild commotion, That peaceful stillness reigneth evermore.

Used by arr. with Oliver Ditson Co., owners of Copyright.

2 Far, far beneath, the noise of tempests dieth,
   And silver waves chime ever peacefully,
   And no rude storm, how fierce so e'er it flieth,
   Disturbs the Sabbath of that deeper sea.

3 So to the heart that knows Thy love, O Purest!
   There is a temple, sacred evermore,
   And all the babble of life's angry voices
   Dies in hushed stillness at its peaceful door.

4 Far, far away, the roar of passion dieth,
   And loving thoughts rise calm and peacefully,
   And no rude storm, how fierce so e'er it flieth,
   Disturbs the soul that dwells, O Lord, in Thee.

162.

1 We would see Jesus—for the shadows lengthen
   Across this little landscape of our life;
  We would see Jesus, our weak faith to strengthen
   For the last weariness—the final strife.

2 We would see Jesus—the great Rock Foundation,
   Whereon our feet were set with sovereign grace;
  Not life, nor death, with all their agitation,
   Can thence remove us, if we see His face.

3 We would see Jesus—this is all we're needing,
   Strength, joy, and willingness come with the sight;
  We would see Jesus, dying, risen, pleading,
   Then welcome day, and farewell mortal night!

Trust.

163. Trust in God, and do the Right.

NORMAN MACLEOD.   DARIUS E. JONES.

1. Cour-age, broth-er! do not stum-ble, Tho' thy path be dark as night;
There's a Star to guide the hum-ble, "Trust in God, and do the right."

2 Let the road be rough and dreary,
   And the end far out of sight;
Foot it bravely, strong or weary,
   "Trust in God, and do the right."

3 Some will hate thee, some will love thee
   Some will flatter, some will slight,
Cease from man, and look above thee,
   "Trust in God, and do the right."

164.

1 Silently the shades of evening
   Gather round my lowly door;
Silently they bring before me
   Faces I shall see no more.

2 O the lost, the unforgotten,
   Though the world be oft forgot!
O the shrouded and the lonely,
   In our hearts they perish not!

3 Living in the silent hours,
   Where our spirits only blend,
They, unlinked with earthly trouble,
   We, still hoping for its end.

4 How such holy memories cluster,
   Like the stars when storms are past,
Pointing up to that fair heaven
   We may hope to gain at last.

                    Christopher C. Cox.

167. Light at Evening-time.

RICHARD H. ROBINSON.   F. FILITZ.

1. Ho-ly Fa-ther, cheer our way With Thy love's per-pet-ual ray: Grant us ev - 'ry clos - ing day Light at evening-time.
2. Ho-ly Sav-iour, calm our fears When earth's brightness disappears: Grant us in our la - ter years Light at evening-time.

3 Holy Spirit, be Thou nigh
   When in mortal pains we lie;
   Grant us, as we come to die,
      Light at evening-time.

4 Holy, blessèd Trinity,
   Darkness is not dark to Thee;
   Those Thou keepest always see
      Light at evening-time.

168. Thine for Ever! God of Love!

Mrs. MARY F. MAUDE.   CHARLES THIRTLE.

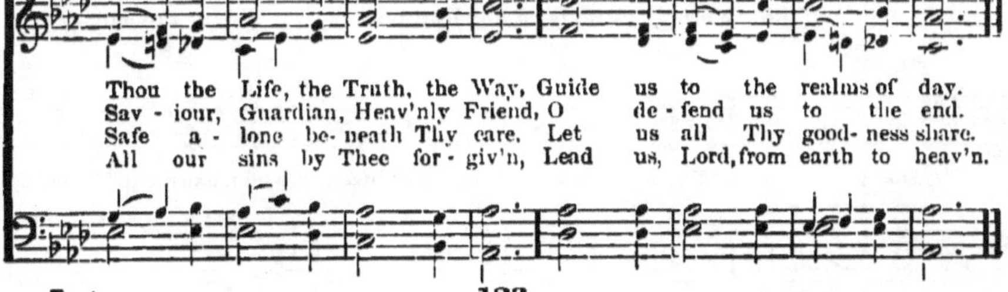

1. Thine for ev - er! God of love! Hear us from Thy throne a - bove; Thou the Life, the Truth, the Way, Guide us to the realms of day.
2. Thine for ev - er! oh, how blest They who find in Thee their rest; Sav - iour, Guardian, Heav'nly Friend, O de - fend us to the end.
3. Thine for ev - er! Sav - iour keep Us, Thy frail and trem-bling sheep; Safe a - lone be - neath Thy care, Let us all Thy good-ness share.
4. Thine for ev - er! Thou our Guide, All our wants by Thee sup-plied; All our sins by Thee for - giv'n, Lead us, Lord, from earth to heav'n.

Trust.

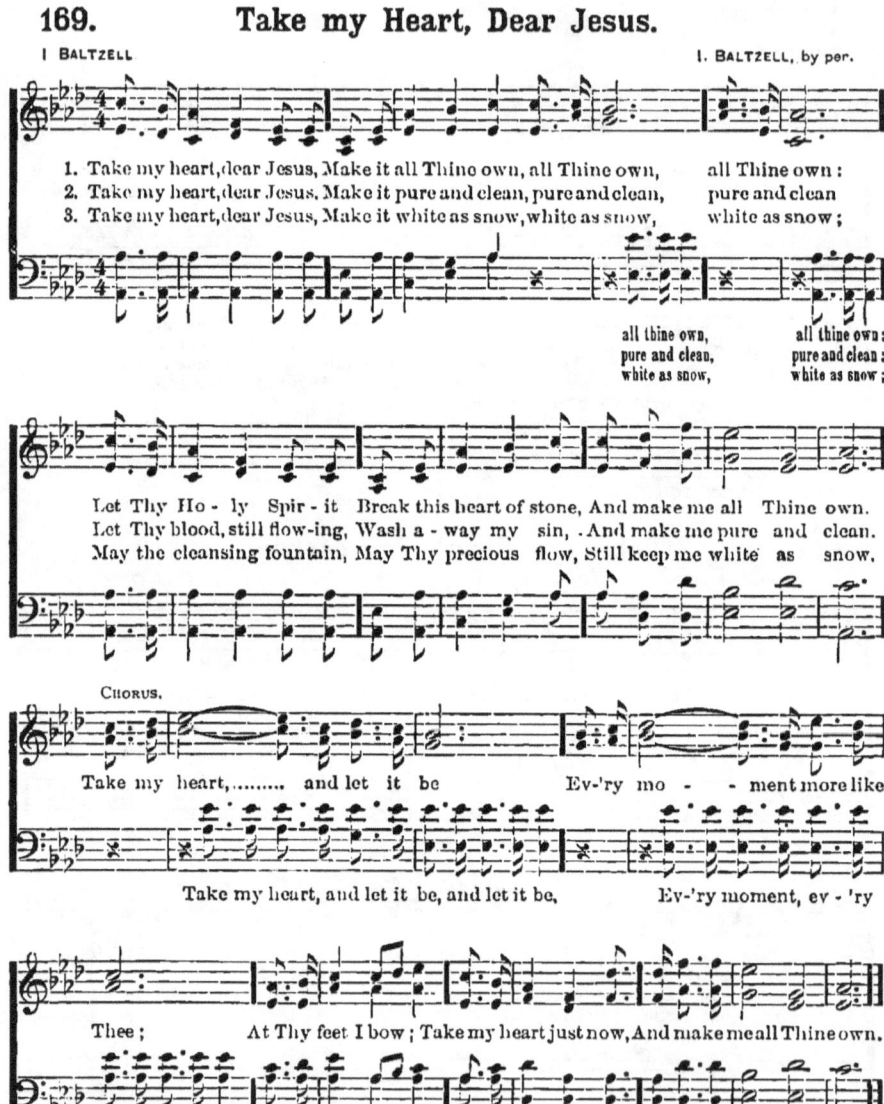

170. Come, let us All Unite.

RICHARD JUKES.   Anon.

1. Come, let us all unite and sing, God is love, God is love, Let heav'n and earth their praises bring— God is love, God is love. Let ev'ry soul from sin awake, Each in his heart sweet music make, And sing with us, for Jesus' sake, God is love, God is love.
2. Oh! tell to earth's remotest bound, God is love, God is love, In Christ we have redemption found— God is love, God is love. His blood hath washed our sins away, His Spirit turn'd our night to day, And led our souls with joy to say, God is love, God is love.
3. How happy is our portion here— God is love, God is love. His promises our spirits cheer— God is love, God is love. He is our sun and shield by day, Our help, our hope, our strength and stay,— He will be with us all the way— God is love, God is love.
4. In glory we shall sing again, God is love, God is love; Yes, this shall be our lofty strain, God is love, God is love. While endless ages roll along, In concert with the heavenly throng, This shall be still our sweetest song, God is love, God is love.

171.

1 My heart is fixed, immortal God,
    Fixed on Thee, fixed on Thee!
And my eternal choice is made,
    Christ for me, Christ for me!
He is my Prophet, Priest and King,
Who did for me salvation bring,
And while I breathe I mean to sing,
    "Christ for me, Christ for me!"

2 Let others boast of heaps of gold,
    Christ for me, Christ for me!
His riches never can be told,
    Christ for me, Christ for me

Your gold will waste and wear away,
Your honor perish in a day,
My portion never can decay;
    Christ for me, Christ for me!

3 In pining sickness or in health,
    Christ for me, Christ for me!
In deepest poverty or wealth,
    Christ for me, Christ for me!
And in that all-important day,
When I the summons must obey,
And pass from this dark world away;
    Christ for me, Christ for me!

Consecration.

173. I Bring my Sins to Thee.

FRANCES R. HAVERGAL.   Anon.

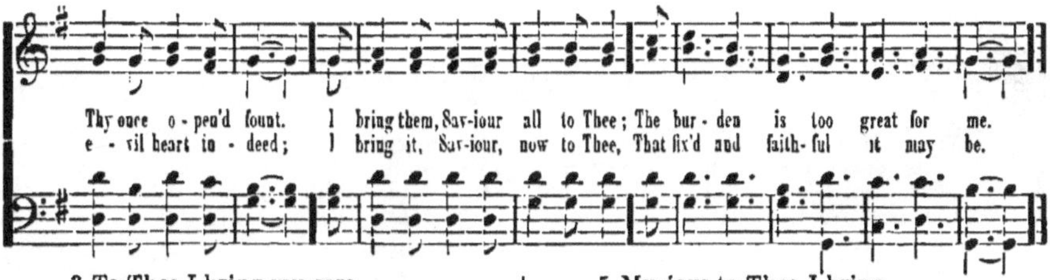

1. I bring my sins to Thee, The sins I can-not count, That all may cleans-ed be At Thy once o-pen'd fount. I bring them, Sav-iour all to Thee; The bur-den is too great for me.
2. My heart to Thee I bring, The heart I can-not read, A faith-less wand'ring thing, An e-vil heart in-deed; I bring it, Sav-iour, now to Thee, That fix'd and faith-ful it may be.

3 To Thee I bring my care,
  The care I cannot flee;
Thou wilt not only share,
  But take it all for me.
O loving Saviour! now to Thee,
I bring the load that wearies me.

4 I bring my grief to Thee,
  The grief I cannot tell;
No words shall needed be,
  Thou knowest all so well.
I bring the sorrow laid on me,
O suffering Saviour! all to Thee.

5 My joys to Thee I bring,
  The joys Thy love has given,
That each may be a wing
  To lift me nearer heaven.
I bring them, Saviour, all to Thee,
Who hast procured them all for me.

6 My life I bring to Thee,
  I would not be my own;
O Saviour! let me be
  Thine ever, Thine alone!
My heart, my life, my all I bring
To Thee, my Saviour and my King.

174. Thine, Lord, Forever.

WILLIAM BENNETT.   HUBERT P. MAIN.

1. Thine, Lord, for-ev-er, Pur-chas'd by blood di-vine; Res-cued and sav'd by Thee, Lord, I am Thine.
2. Thine, Lord, for-ev-er, Tho' death shall lay me low; E'en in that dread-ful hour, Thine, Lord, I know.
3. Thine, Lord, for-ev-er, When safe be-fore Thy throne I stand, for-ev-er-more Thine, Thine a-lone.

Copyright, 1889, by Biglow & Main.

Consecration.

175. Peace, be Still!

GODFREY THRING.   J. B. DYKES.

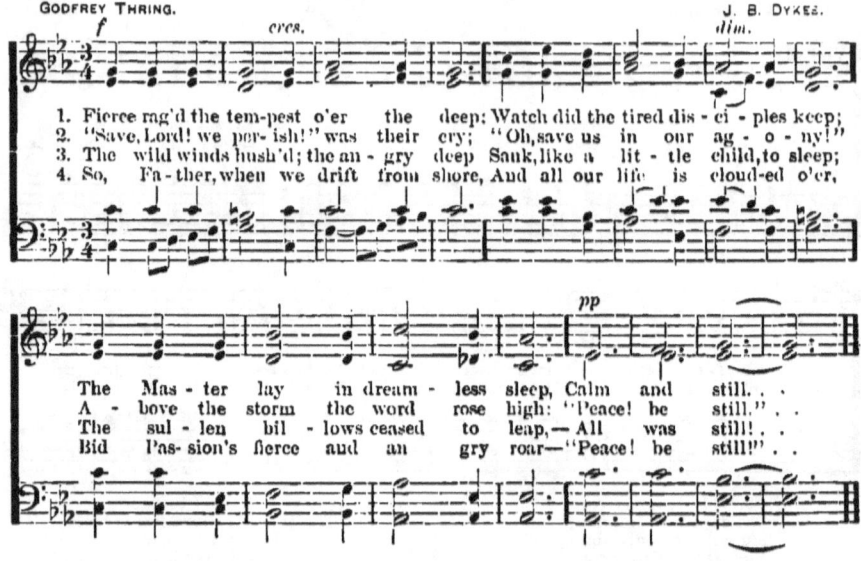

1. Fierce rag'd the tem-pest o'er the deep; Watch did the tired dis-ci-ples keep;
2. "Save, Lord! we per-ish!" was their cry; "Oh, save us in our ag-o-ny!"
3. The wild winds hush'd; the an-gry deep Sank, like a lit-tle child, to sleep;
4. So, Fa-ther, when we drift from shore, And all our life is cloud-ed o'er,

The Mas-ter lay in dream-less sleep, Calm and still.
A - bove the storm the word rose high: "Peace! be still."
The sul - len bil - lows ceased to leap,— All was still!
Bid Pas-sion's fierce and an - gry roar—"Peace! be still!"

176. Breathe on Me, Breath of God.

EDWIN HATCH.   J. B. CALKIN.

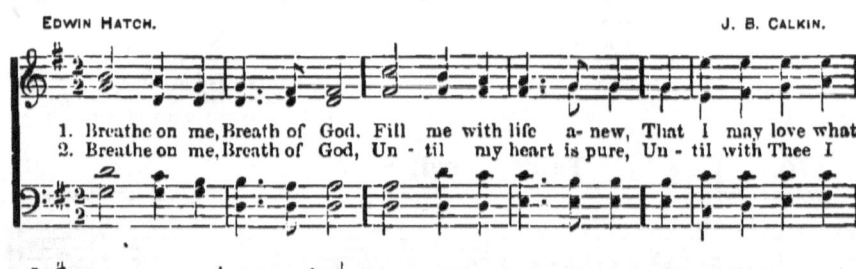

1. Breathe on me, Breath of God, Fill me with life a-new, That I may love what
2. Breathe on me, Breath of God, Un-til my heart is pure, Un-til with Thee I

Thou dost love, And do what Thou wouldst do.
will one will, To do or to en-dure.

3 Breathe on me, Breath of God,
Till I am wholly Thine,
Till all this earthly part of me
Glows with Thy fire divine.

4 Breathe on me, Breath of God,
So shall I never die,
But live with Thee the perfect life
Of Thine eternity.

Consecration.

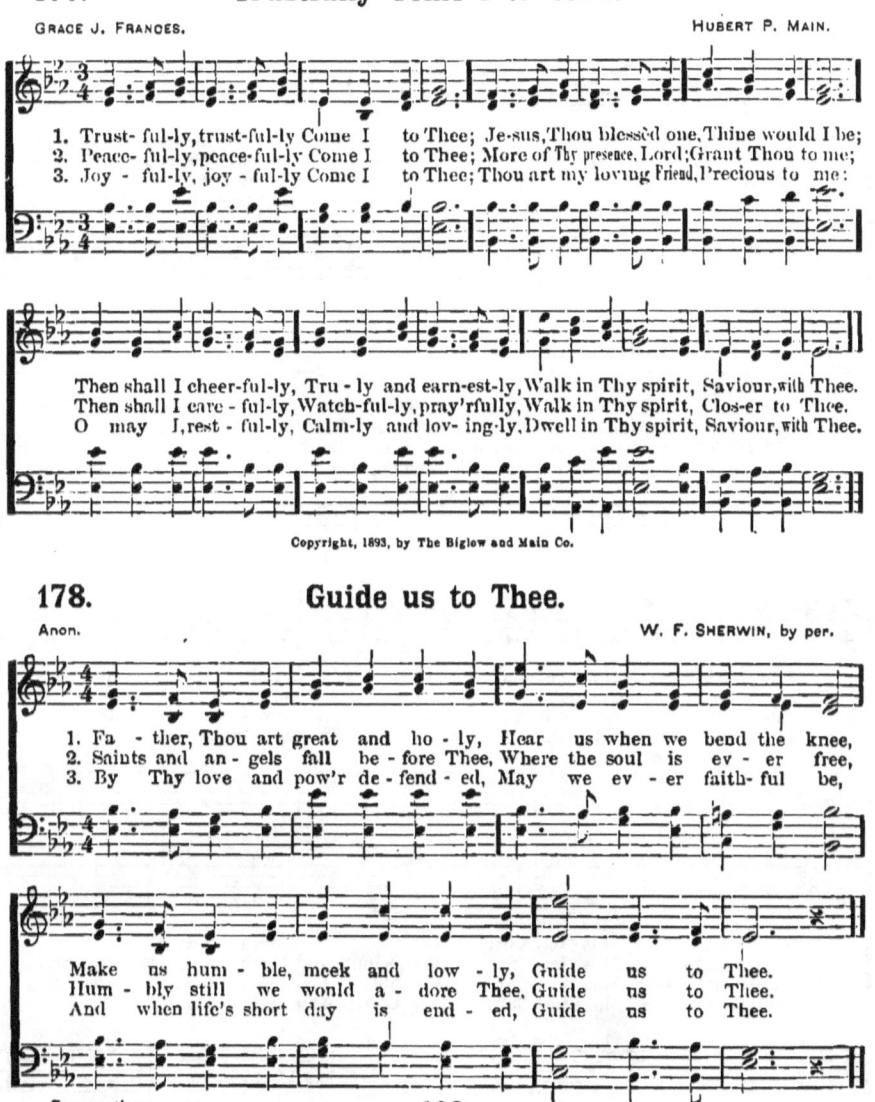

180. Bringing in the Sheaves.

KNOWLES SHAW. GEORGE A. MINOR.

1. Sow-ing in the morn-ing, sow-ing seeds of kind-ness, Sow-ing in the noon-tide and the dew-y eve;
2. Sow-ing in the sun-shine, sow-ing in the shad-ow, Fear-ing neith-er clouds nor win-ter's chill-ing breeze;
3. Go-ing forth with weep-ing, sow-ing for the Mas-ter, Tho' the loss sus-tained our spir-it oft-en grieves;

Wait-ing for the har-vest, and the time of reap-ing, We shall come re-joic-ing, bring-ing in the sheaves.
By and by the har-vest, and the la-bor end-ed, We shall come re-joic-ing, bring-ing in the sheaves.
When our weep-ing's o-ver, He will bid us wel-come, We shall come re-joic-ing, bring-ing in the sheaves.

CHORUS.

Bring-ing in the sheaves, bring-ing in the sheaves, We shall come re-joic-ing, bring-ing in the sheaves.

Bring-ing in the sheaves, bring-ing in the sheaves, We shall come re-joic-ing, bring-ing in the sheaves.

Used by permission.

Christian Endeavor.

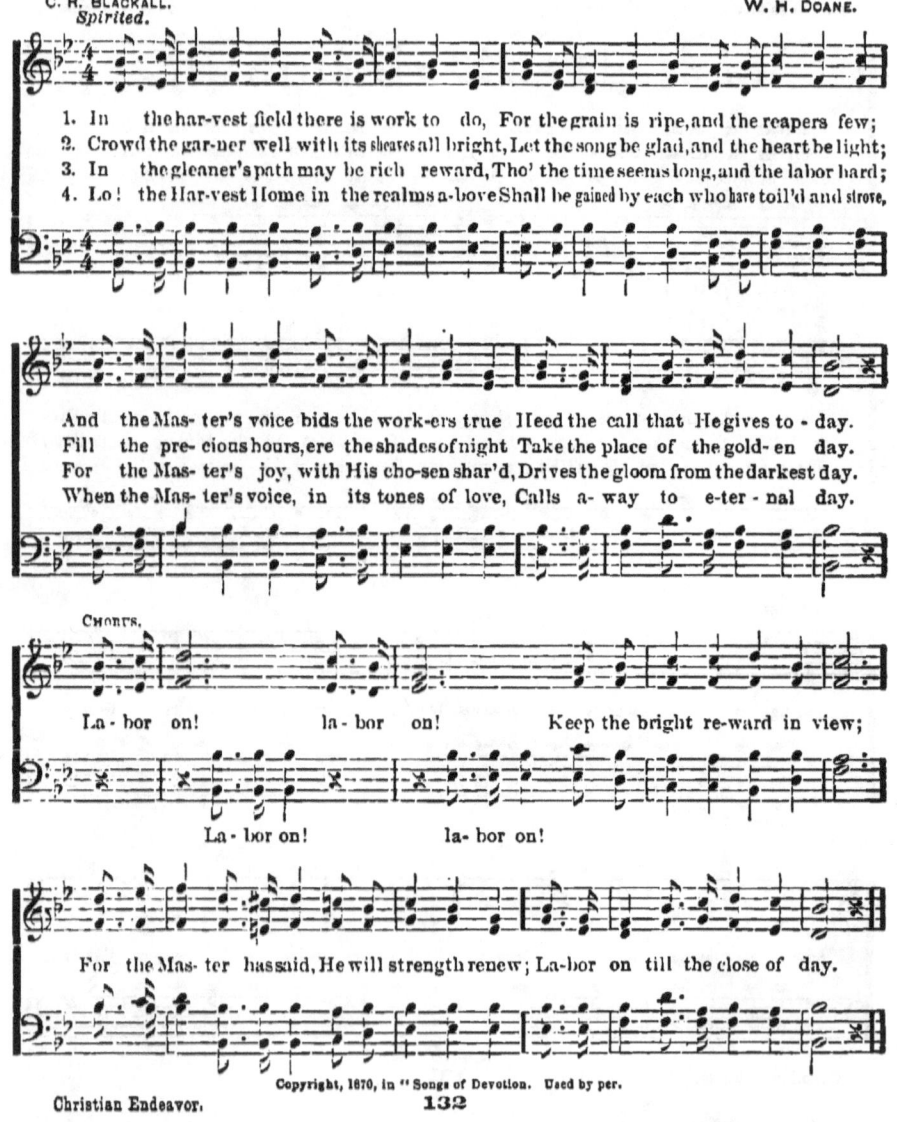

182. God Speed the Right.

W. E. Hickson.   German.

1. Now to Heav'n our pray'r as-cend-ing, God speed the right; In a no-ble cause con-tend-ing, God speed the right. Be our zeal in Heav'n re-cord-ed, With suc-cess on Earth re-ward-ed, God speed the right, God speed the right.

2. Be that pray'r a-gain re-peat-ed, God speed the right; Ne'er de-spair-ing, tho' de-feat-ed, God speed the right. Like the good and great in sto-ry, If we fail, we fail with glo-ry, God speed the right, God speed the right.

3. Pa-tient, firm, and per-se-ver-ing, God speed the right; Ne'er th' e-vent nor dan-ger fear-ing, God speed the right. Pain, nor toil, nor tri-al heed-ing, In the strength of Heav'n suc-ceed-ing— God speed the right, God speed the right.

4 Still our onward course pursuing
   God speed the right;
Ev'ry foe at length subduing,
   God speed the right;
Truth our cause, whate'er delay it,
There's no power on earth can stay it;
   ‖: God speed the right. :‖

Christian Endeavor.

183. The Sowers.

Anon.
Rev. Geo. G. Phipps.

1. Ten thousand sowers thro' the land, Pass'd heedless on their way; Ten thousand seeds in ev-'ry hand, Of ev-'ry sort had they. They cast seed here, they cast seed there, They cast seed ev'ry-where. Ten thousand seeds in ev-'ry hand, They cast seed ev'ry-where.
2. A-non as many a year went by, Those sowers came once more, And wander'd 'neath the leaf-hid sky, And wonder'd at the store; For fruit hung here, and fruit hung there, And fruit hung ev'ry-where. And each one wonder'd at the store, For fruit hung ev'ry-where.
3. Nor knew they in that tangled wood The trees that were their own; Yet as they pluck'd, as each one should, Each pluck'd what he had sown. So do men here, so do men there, So do men ev-'ry-where. For each one pluck'd what he had sown, So do men ev'ry-where.

Copyright, 1884, by F. N. Peloubet.

184.

1 The banner cross is waving high,
  The standard of our God,
 To arms, to arms!—the battle cry—
  Ring out the cheering-word.
 There's sound of victory in the air,
  And shout of triumph grand;
 The hosts of God in mighty prayer
  Are sweeping through the land.

2 The hand of faith lays hold of God,
  And chokes the springs of death,
 And pours the streams of life abroad,
  To sweeten poison's breath.
 March on! march on! ye conquering hosts,
  Till not a foe shall stand,
 Nor haunt of vice through all our coasts,
  Nor drunkard in the land.

Rev. F. Bottome.

Christian Endeavor.

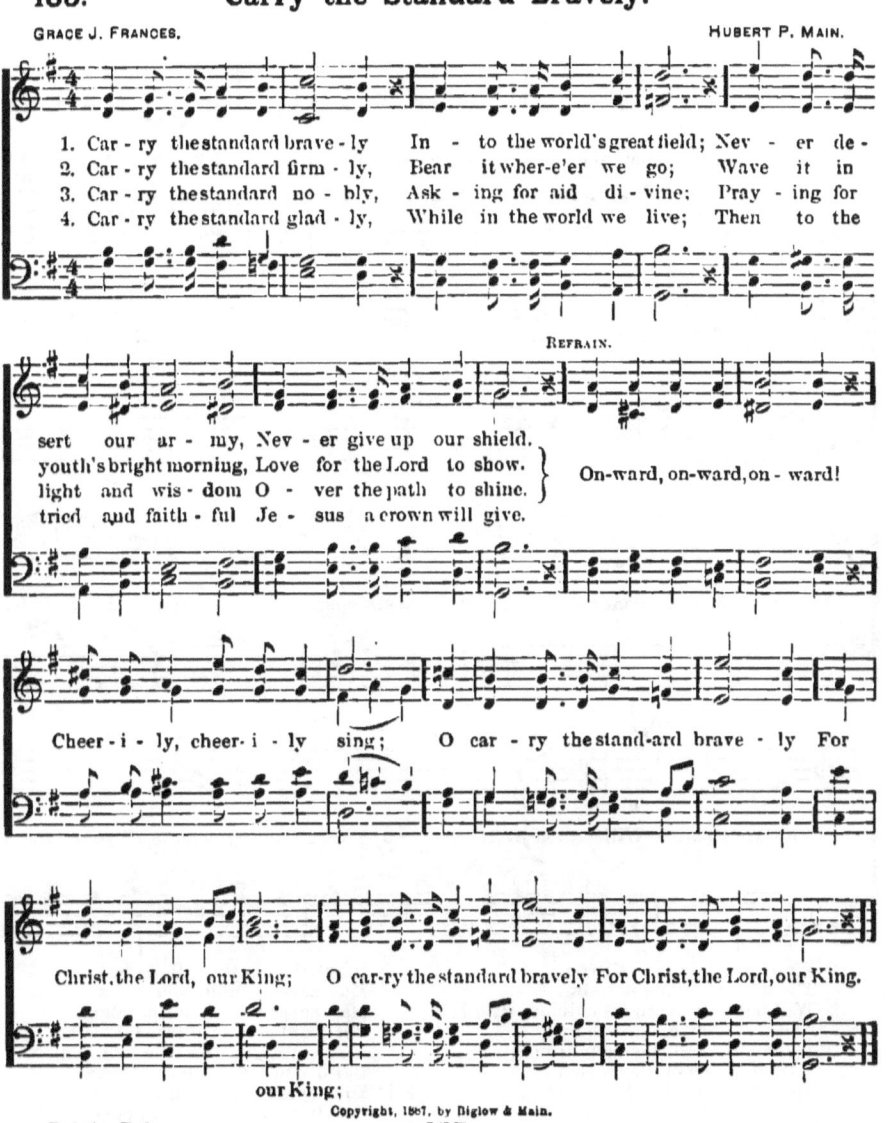

186. Strive, Wait, and Pray.

Tr. by ADELAIDE A. PROCTER.   HENRY FARMER.

1. Strive! yet I do not promise The prize you dream of to-day, Will not fade when you think to grasp it, And melt in your hand a-way; But an-oth-er and ho-li-er treas-ure, You would now perchance dis-dain, Will come when your toil is o-ver, And pay you for all your pain,—Will come when your toil is o-ver, And pay you for all your pain.

2 Wait! yet I do not tell you
The hour you long for now
Will not come with its radiance vanish'd,
And a shadow upon its brow;
Yet far through the misty future,
With a crown of starry light,
‖: An hour of joy you know not
Is winging her silent flight. :‖

3 Pray! though the gift you ask for
May never comfort your fears,
May never repay your pleading,
Yet pray, and with hopeful tears;
An answer, not that you long for,
But diviner, will come one day,
‖: Your eyes are too dim to see it;
Yet strive, and wait, and pray. :‖

Christian Endeavor.

187. Resting in God's Love.

C. R. Hagenback, tr. by H. A. P.
Arr. by Hubert P. Main.

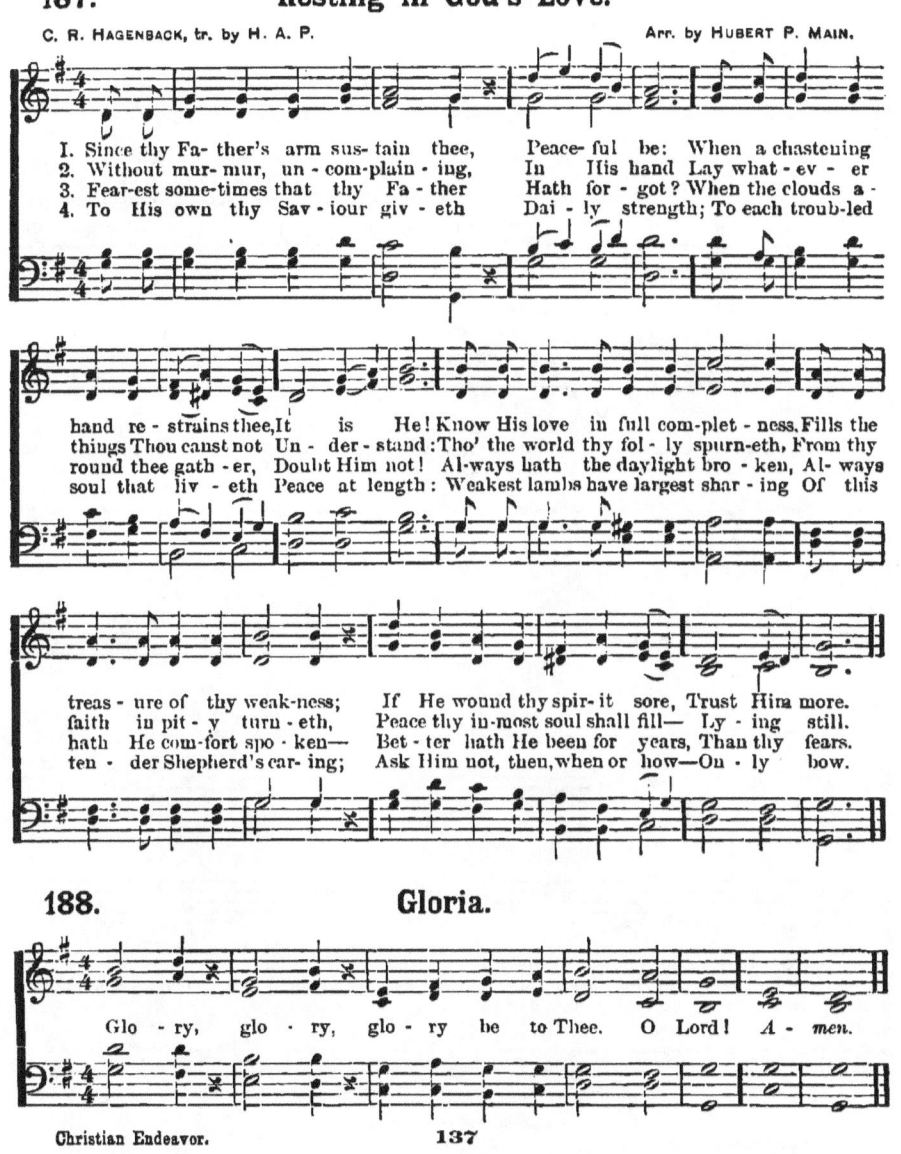

1. Since thy Fa-ther's arm sus-tain thee, Peace-ful be: When a chastening hand re-strains thee, It is He! Know His love in full com-plet-ness, Fills the treas-ure of thy weak-ness; If He wound thy spir-it sore, Trust Him more.
2. Without mur-mur, un-com-plain-ing, In His hand Lay what-ev-er things Thou canst not Un-der-stand: Tho' the world thy fol-ly spurn-eth, From thy faith in pit-y turn-eth, Peace thy in-most soul shall fill— Ly-ing still.
3. Fear-est some-times that thy Fa-ther Hath for-got? When the clouds a-round thee gath-er, Doubt Him not! Al-ways hath the daylight bro-ken, Al-ways hath He com-fort spo-ken— Bet-ter hath He been for years, Than thy fears.
4. To His own thy Sav-iour giv-eth Dai-ly strength; To each troub-led soul that liv-eth Peace at length: Weakest lambs have largest shar-ing Of this ten-der Shepherd's car-ing; Ask Him not, then, when or how— On-ly bow.

188. Gloria.

Glo - ry, glo - ry, glo - ry be to Thee, O Lord! A - men.

Christian Endeavor.

O Jesus! Lead us Onward.—Concluded.

champions for the Lord; Fling out the roy-al stand-ard, Un-sheath the mighty sword.

190. For Christ is our Endeavor.

Rev. ROBERT F. GORDON.   HUBERT P. MAIN.

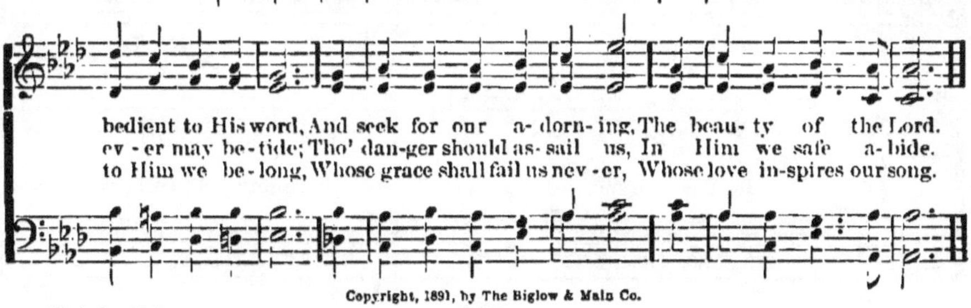

1. For Christ is our En-deav- or, Our hearts to Him be- long; His presence cheers us ev - er, His love in-spires our song; We come in youth's bright morning. O - bedient to His word, And seek for our a- dorn- ing, The beau-ty of the Lord.

2. In full- ness of His bless- ing, Good work for Him we'll do; The band with joy con- fess- ing, His stand-ard-bear- ers true; And He will nev- er fail us, What- ev - er may be-tide; Tho' dan-ger should as- sail us, In Him we safe a- bide.

3. So with youth's ardor glow- ing, We form a Christian band; The mind of Je- sus know- ing, We for His hon - or stand; For He is our En- deav-or, And to Him we be- long, Whose grace shall fail us nev - er, Whose love in-spires our song.

Copyright, 1891, by The Biglow & Main Co.

Christian Endeavor.

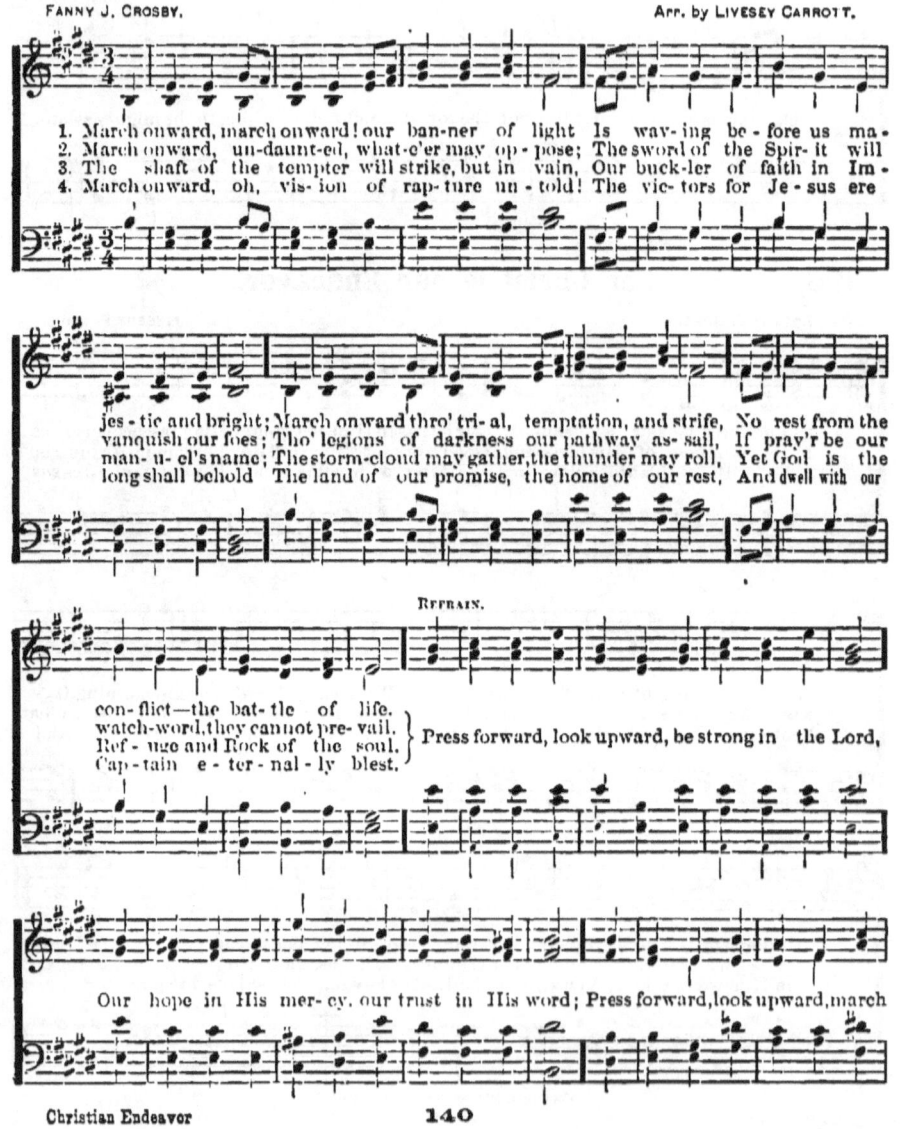

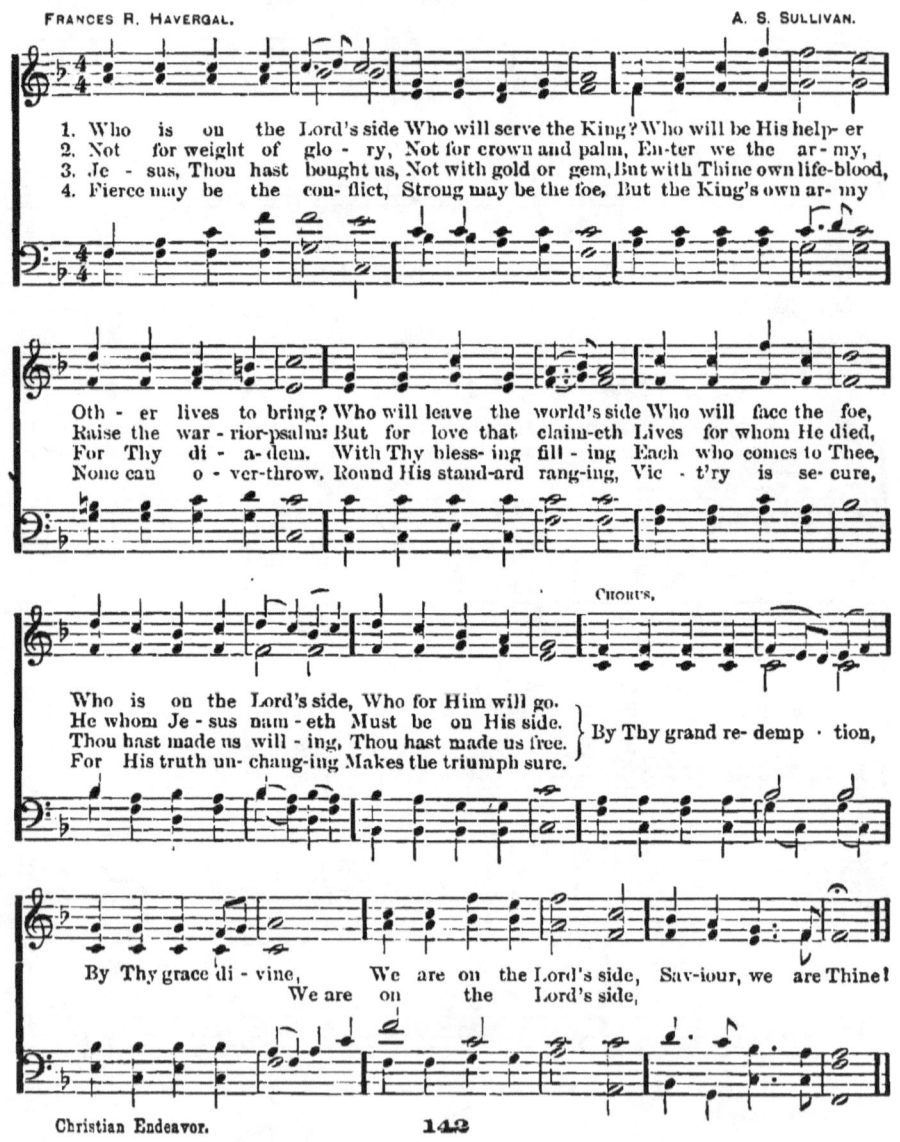

Watch and Pray.—Concluded.

O, watch in the darkness and watch in the day; Chris- tian, watch and pray.

196.   Christian! Dost Thou see Them.

Tr. J. M. NEALE.   J. B. DYKES.

1. Chris-tian! dost thou see them On the ho - ly ground? How the powers of dark-ness Rage thy steps a - round? Chris-tian, up, and smite them! Count-ing gain but loss; In the strength that com- eth By the Ho - ly Cross.
2. Chris-tian! dost thou feel them, How they work with - in, Striv - ing, tempt-ing, lur - ing, Goad-ing in - to sin? Chris-tian, nev - er trem - ble; Nev - er be down-cast; Gird thee for the bat - tle, Watch and pray and fast.
3. "Well I know thy trouble, O My serv-ant true; Thou art ver - y wea - ry, I was wea - ry too; But that toil shall make thee Some day all Mine own, And the end of sor - row Shall be near My throne."

Watchfulness.

199. Dear Lord, Remember Me.

THOMAS HAWEIS
Music, BEETHOVEN.
Arr. G. C. PHIPPS.

1. O Thou, from whom all goodness flows, I lift my soul to Thee; In all my sorrows, conflicts, woes, O Lord, remember me.
2. When, groaning, on my burden'd heart My sins lie heav-i-ly, Thy pardon speak, new peace impart, In love remember me.

3 If, on my face, for Thy dear name,
    Shame and reproaches be,
  All hail reproach, and welcome shame,
    If Thou remember me.

  The hour is near; consigned to death,
    I own the just decree:
  Saviour, with my last parting breath,
    I'll cry, "remember me!"

Copyright, 1893, by Biglow & Main Co.

200. Prayer, the Soul's Desire.

JAS. MONTGOMERY.
THOS. HASTINGS.

1. Pray'r is the soul's sincere de-sire, Un-utter'd or ex-press'd; The mo-tion of a hid-den fire That trembles in the breast.
2. Pray'r is the burden of a sigh, The fall-ing of a tear, The upward glancing of an eye, When none but God is near.
3. Pray'r is the simplest form of speech That infant lips can try; Pray'r, the sublimest strains that reach The Ma-jes-ty on high.
4. Pray'r is the contrite sinner's voice, Re-turn-ing from his ways; While angels in their songs rejoice, And cry, "behold, he prays!"

5 Pray'r is the Christian's vital breath,
    The Christian's native air,
  His watchword at the gates of death;
    He enters heaven with prayer.

6 O Thou, by whom we come to God,
    The Life, the Truth, the Way!
  The path of prayer Thyself hast trod;
    Lord! teach us how to pray.

Prayer.

204. Jesus, Who for us Didst Bear.

R. F. LITTLEDALE.   A. S. SULLIVAN.

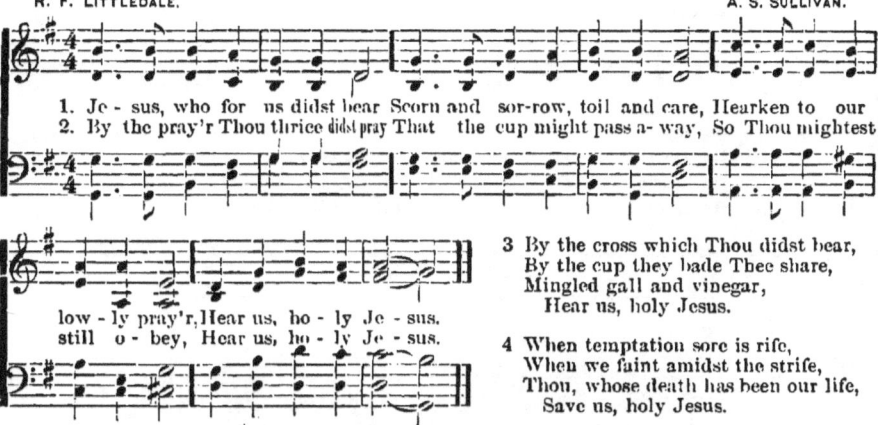

1. Jesus, who for us didst bear Scorn and sorrow, toil and care, Hearken to our lowly pray'r, Hear us, holy Jesus.
2. By the pray'r Thou thrice didst pray That the cup might pass away, So Thou mightest still obey, Hear us, holy Jesus.

3 By the cross which Thou didst bear,
  By the cup they bade Thee share,
  Mingled gall and vinegar,
    Hear us, holy Jesus.

4 When temptation sore is rife,
  When we faint amidst the strife,
  Thou, whose death has been our life,
    Save us, holy Jesus.

205.

1 Light of lights, with morning, shine:
  Lift on us Thy light divine;
  And let charity benign
    Breathe on us her balm.

2 Light of lights, when falls the even.
  Let it close on sin forgiven;
  Fold us in the peace of heaven,
    Shed a holy calm.

3 Ruler of the earth and sea,
  Dimly here we worship Thee:
  With the saints hereafter we
    Hope to bear the palm.
          Gilbert Rorison.

206.

1 Lord of mercy and of might,
  Of mankind the life and light,
  Maker, teacher, infinite,
    Jesus, hear and save.

2 Mighty monarch! Saviour mild!
  Humbled to a mortal child,
  Captive, beaten, bound, reviled,
    Jesus, hear and save.

3. Throned above celestial things,
  Borne aloft on angels, wings,
  Lord of lords, and King of kings,
    Jesus, hear and save.

Prayer.

4 Soon to come to earth again,
  Judge of angels and of men.
  Hear us now, and hear us then,
    Jesus, hear and save.
          Reginald Heber.

207.

1 God of pity, God of grace,
  When we humbly seek Thy face,
  Bend from heaven, Thy dwelling place;
    Hear, forgive and save.

2 When we in Thy temple meet,
  Spread our wants before Thy feet,
  Pleading at Thy mercy-seat;
    Look from heaven and save.

3 When Thy love our hearts shall fill,
  And we long to do Thy will,
  Turning to Thy holy hill:
    Lord, accept and save.

4 Should we wander from Thy fold,
  And our love to Thee grow cold,
  With a pitying eye behold;
    Lord, forgive and save.

5 Should the hand of sorrow press,
  Earthly care and want distress,
  May our souls Thy peace possess;
    Jesus, hear and save.

6 And whate'er our cry may be,
  When we lift our hearts to Thee,
  From our burden set us free:
    Hear, forgive and save.
          Eliza Fanny Morris.

208. Jesus from Thy Throne on High.

THOS. B. POLLOCK. F. A. J. HERVEY.

1. Jesus, from Thy throne on high, Far above the bright blue sky;
   Look on us with loving eye;
   Hear us, Holy Jesus!
2. Little children need not fear, When they know that Thou art near;
   Thou dost love us, Saviour dear;
   Hear us, Holy Jesus!
3. Little hearts may love Thee well, Little lips Thy love may tell,
   Little hymns Thy praises swell;
   Hear us, Holy Jesus!
4. Little lives may be divine, Little deeds of love may shine,
   Little ones be wholly Thine;
   Hear us, Holy Jesus!

209.

1 Jesus, David's Root and Stem,
Jesus, Bright and glorious Gem,
Jesus, Babe of Bethlehem;
Hear us, Holy Jesus.

2 Jesus, at whose infant Feet,
Shepherds, coming Thee to greet,
Knelt to pay their worship meet;
Hear us, Holy Jesus.

3 Jesus, unto whom of yore
Wise men, hastening to adore,
Gold and myrrh and incense bore;
Hear us, Holy Jesus.

4 From all childish sins that stain,
From all words that might give pain,
From all evil thoughts and vain;
Save us, Holy Jesus.

5 From each proud and sullen mood,
From all tempers rough and rude,
Hardness and ingratitude;
Save us, Holy Jesus.

6 From a will that disobeys,
From all selfish works and ways,
From all guile and falsehood base;
Save us, Holy Jesus.

7 By Thy Pattern bright and pure,
By the pains Thou did'st endure
Our salvation to procure;
Save us, Holy Jesus.

R. F. Littledale.

210.

1 Heavenly Father let Thy light
Break upon our blinded sight,
Chase away the shades of night,
We beseech Thee, hear us.

Prayer.

2 Jesus, who did'st suffer pain,
To release from error's chain;
Man's lost Paradise to gain,
Jesus, Saviour, hear us.

3 Seek for those who careless roam,
Bring the wanderers safely home,

May Thy glorious kingdom come
Jesus, Saviour, hear us.

4 Come and bring new life within,
Rescue souls from death and sin,
Teach the careless heaven to win,
Blessed Spirit, hear us.
                                    Anon.

211.   Lord for To-morrow.
(BEYROUT.)

Canon ERNEST R. WILBERFORCE.　　　　　　　　MILLS WHITTLESEY.

1. Lord, for to-morrow and its needs I do not pray:
   Keep me, my God, from stain of sin, Just for to-day.
2. Let me both diligently work And duly pray;
   Let me be kind in word and deed, Just for to-day.
3. Let me be slow to do my will Prompt to obey;
   Help me to mortify my flesh, Just for to-day.

Copyright, 1890, by Mills Whittlesey. From "Harmony and Praise," by per.

4 Let me no wrong or idle word
   Unthinking say;
   Set Thou a seal upon my lips,
   Just for to-day.

5 Let me in season, Lord, be grave—
   In season gay;
   Let me be faithful to Thy grace,
   Just for to-day.

6 And if to-day from earth my life
   Should ebb away,
   Give me my Saviour's presence sweet,
   Just for to-day.

7 So for to-morrow and its needs
   I do not pray;
   But keep me, guide me, love me, Lord,
   Just for to-day.

Prayer.

212. May We Be One.

CHRISTOPHER WORDSWORTH, 1862. Rev. J. B. DYKES.

1. Father of all, from land and sea The nations sing, "Thine, Lord, are we, Countless in number but in Thee May we be one."
2. O Son of God, whose love so free For men did make Thee Man to be, United to our God in Thee, May we be one.
3. Join high and low, join young and old, In love that never waxes cold; Under one Shepherd, in one fold, Make us all one.
4. So, when the world shall pass away, May we awake with joy and say, "Now in the bliss of endless day We are all one."

213.

1 My God! is any hour so sweet,
From blush of morn to evening star,
As that which calls me to Thy feet—
The hour of prayer.

2 Then is my strength by Thee renewed;
Then are my sins by Thee forgiven;
Then dost Thou cheer my solitude
With hopes of heaven.

3 No words can tell what blest relief
There for my every want I find,
What strength for warfare, balm for grief;
What peace of mind.

4 Hushed is each doubt; gone every fear,
My spirit seems in heaven to stay;
And e'en the penitential tear
Is wiped away.

5 Lord, till I reach yon blissful shore
No privilege so dear shall be,
As thus my inmost soul to pour
In prayer to Thee;

214. Lord, Abide with me.

FANNY J. CROSBY. SYLVESTER MAIN.

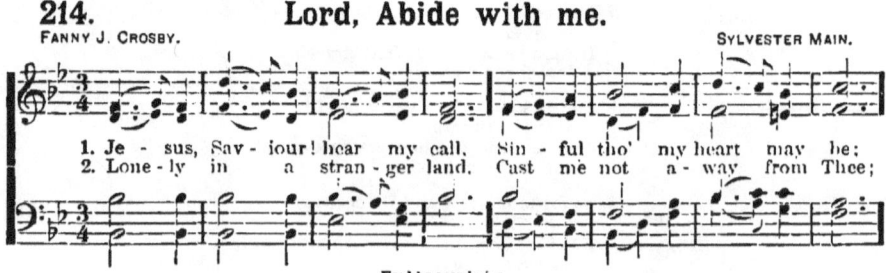

1. Jesus, Saviour! hear my call, Sinful tho' my heart may be;
2. Lonely in a stranger land. Cast me not away from Thee;

Used by permission.

Prayer.

Lord, Abide with me.—Concluded.

Thou, my life, my hope, my all, Lord, a-bide with me.
Lead me by Thy gen-tle hand, Lord, a-bide with me.

3 Thou hast died the lost to save,
  Died to set the captive free;
  Thou didst triumph o'er the grave
  Lord, abide with me.

4 Fill me with Thy love divine,
  Consecrate my life to Thee;
  Bend my stubborn will to Thine,
  Lord, abide with me.

5 When the shades of death prevail,
  Father, let me cling to Thee;
  When I pass the gloomy vale,
  Lord, abide with me.

6 Then, oh! then, my raptured soul
  Heaven's eternal rest shall see;
  There, while endless ages roll,
  Live and reign with me.

215.

1 Holy Ghost, the infinite,
  Shine upon our nature's night
  With Thy blessed inward light,
  Comforter Divine!

2 We are sinful, cleanse us, Lord;
  We are faint, Thy strength afford,
  Lost, until by Thee restored,
  Comforter Divine!

3 Like the dew, Thy peace distil;
  Guide, subdue our wayward will,
  Things of Christ unfolding still,
  Comforter Divine!

4 Holy Ghost! the infinite,
  Shine upon our nature's night
  With Thy blessed inward light,
  Comforter Divine!

George Rawson.

216. Only One Prayer To-day.
Rev. W. C. Dix. L. M. Fosberry.

1. On-ly one pray'r to-day, One earn-est, tear-ful plea;
2. Al-though my sin is great, Still to my God I flee;
3. No oth-er Name than His, My hope, my help may be:

A lit-a-ny from out the heart— Have mer-cy, Lord, on me.
Yes, I can dare look up and say, Have mer-cy, Lord, on me.
Oh, by that one all-sav-ing Name, Have mer-cy, Lord, on me.

Prayer.

217. From the Recesses.

Sir JOHN BOWRING.   F. F. FLEMMING.

1. From the recesses of a lowly spirit,
Our humble pray'r ascends, O Father, hear it;
Borne on the trembling wings of fear and meekness,
Forgive its weakness.

2. We know, we feel how mean, and how unworthy
The lowly sacrifice we pour before Thee:
What can we offer Thee: O Thou most holy!
But sin and folly.

3 We see Thy hand, it leads us, it supports us:
We hear Thy voice, it counsels, and it courts us:
And then we turn away! yet still Thy kindness
Forgives our blindness.

4 Who can resist Thy gentle call, appealing
To every generous thought and grateful feeling;
Oh! who can hear the accents of Thy mercy,
And never love Thee.

5 Kind Benefactor! plant within this bosom
The seeds of holiness, and let them blossom
In fragrance, and in beauty bright and vernal,
And spring eternal.

6 Then place them in those everlasting gardens
Where angels walk, and seraphs are the wardens;
Where every flower, brought safe through death's dark portal,
Becomes immortal.

Prayer.

218.

1 Now God be with us, for the night is closing;
The light and darkness are of His disposing,
And 'neath His shadow we to rest may yield us,
For He will shield us.

2 Let evil thoughts and spirits flee before us;
Till morning cometh, watch, O Father o'er us;
In soul and body Thou from harm defend us;
Thine angels send us.

3 Let holy thoughts be ours when sleep o'ertake us;
Our earliest thoughts be Thine when morning [wakes us,
Serve Thee all day; in all that we are doing
Thy praise pursuing.

4 Father, Thy name be praised, Thy kingdom given;
Thy will be done on earth, as 'tis in heaven;
Keep us in life, forgive our sins, deliver
Us, now and ever.

C. J. B. Bunsen, tr.

219. From Every Stormy Wind.

Rev. H. STOWELL.   SOLON WILDER.

1. From ev-'ry stormy wind that blows, From ev-'ry swell-ing tide of woes,
There is a calm, a sure re-treat; 'Tis found be-neath the mer-cy-seat.

2 There is a place, where Jesus sheds
The oil of gladness on our heads,—
A place, than all besides, more sweet;
It is the blood-bought mercy-seat.

3 There is a scene where spirits blend,
Where friend holds fellowship with friend;
Though sundered far, by faith they meet
Around one common mercy-seat.

4 There, there, on eagle wings we soar,
And sense and sin molest no more,
And heaven comes down our souls to greet,
And glory crowns the mercy-seat.

Prayer.

220. Prayer, Sweet Prayer.
(QUARTET OR CHOIR.)

Anon. *Prayerfully.*   J. E. GOULD.

1. When torn is the bo-som with sor-row and care, Be it ev-er so sim-ple there's noth-ing like pray'r; It cas-es and soft-ens, sub-dues, yet sus-tains, Gives vig-or to hope and puts pas-sion in chains.
2. When pleas-ure would woo us from pi-e-ty's arms, The si-ren sing sweet-ly or si-lent-ly charms; We list-en, love, loi-ter, and caught in the snare; In look-ing to Je-sus we con-quer by prayer.

REFRAIN. WHOLE SCHOOL.

Prayer, prayer, O sweet prayer, Be it ev-er so sim-ple there's nothing like prayer.

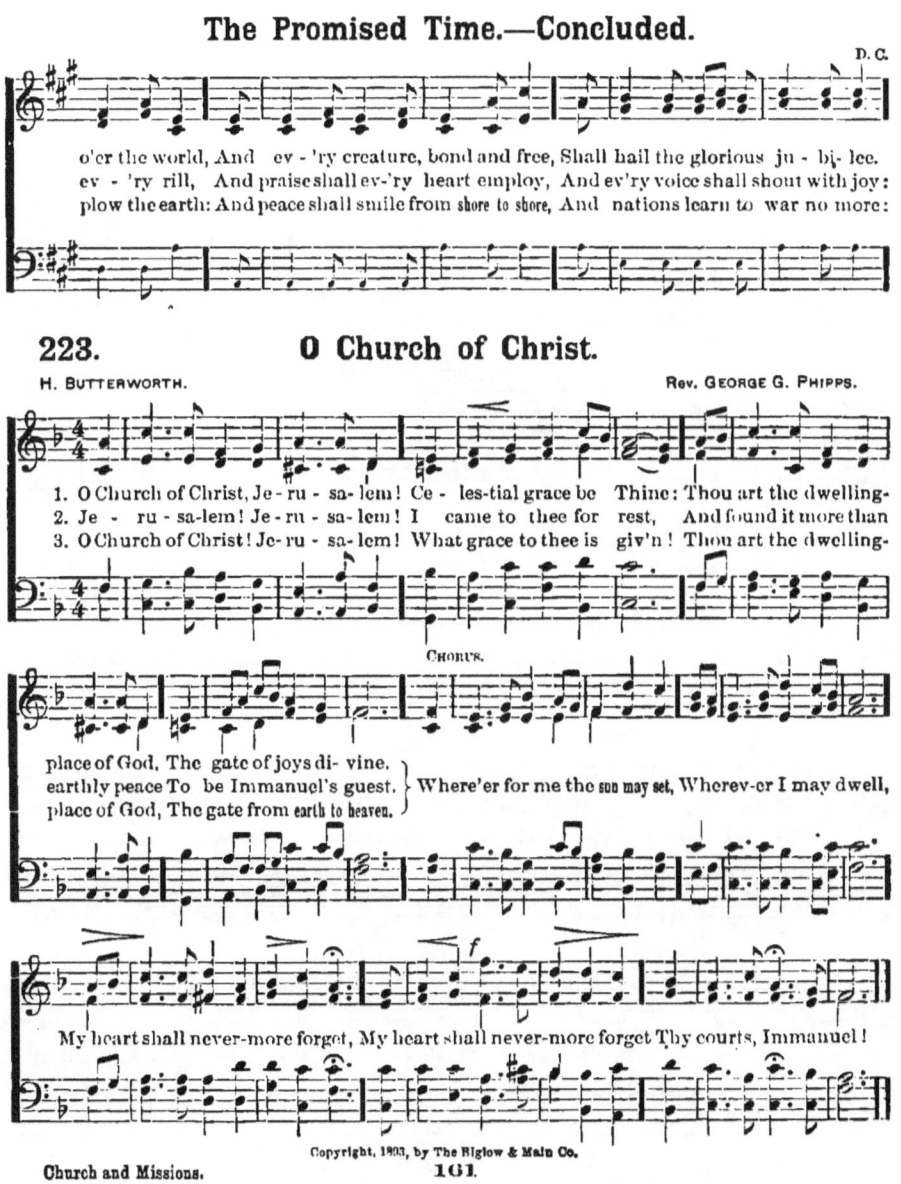

Missionary's Call.—Concluded.

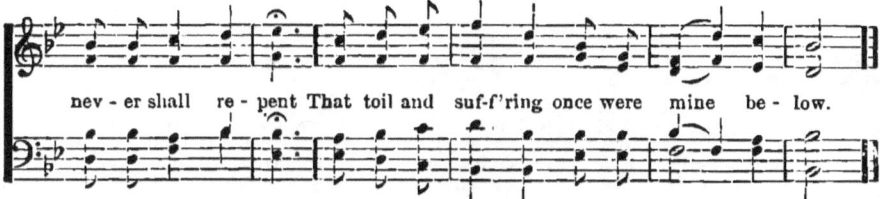

nev-er shall re-pent That toil and suf-f'ring once were mine be-low.

225. On the Mountain's Top.

THOS. KELLY. THOS. HASTINGS.

1. { On the mountain's top ap-pear-ing, Lo! the sacred her-ald stands,
   { Welcome news to Zi-on bear-ing, Zi-on long in hos-tile lands: } Mourning captive!
   God Himself will loose thy bands. Mourning captive! God Himself will loose thy bands.

2 Has thy night been long and mournful!
  Have thy friends unfaithful proved?
  Have thy foes been proud and scornful,
  By thy sighs and tears unmoved?
  ||: Cease thy mourning!
  Zion still is well beloved. :||

3 God, thy God, will now restore thee,
  He Himself appears thy friend;
  All thy foes shall flee before thee,
  Here their boasts and triumphs end
  ||: Great deliverance
  Zion's King vouchsafes to send. :||

226.

1 O'er the gloomy hills of darkness
  Look, my soul, be still,—and gaze;
  See the promises advancing
  To a glorious day of grace:
  ||: Blessèd jubilee!
  Let thy glorious morning dawn. :||

2 Kingdoms wide that sit in darkness—
  Grant them, Lord, the glorious light;
  Now, from eastern coast to western,
  May the morning chase the night;
  ||: Let redemption,
  Freely purchased, win the day. :||

3 Fly abroad, thou mighty gospel!
  Win and conquer,—never cease;
  May thy lasting, wide dominions
  Multiply and still increase:
  ||: Sway the scepter,
  Saviour! all the world around. :||

W. Williams.

Church and Missions.

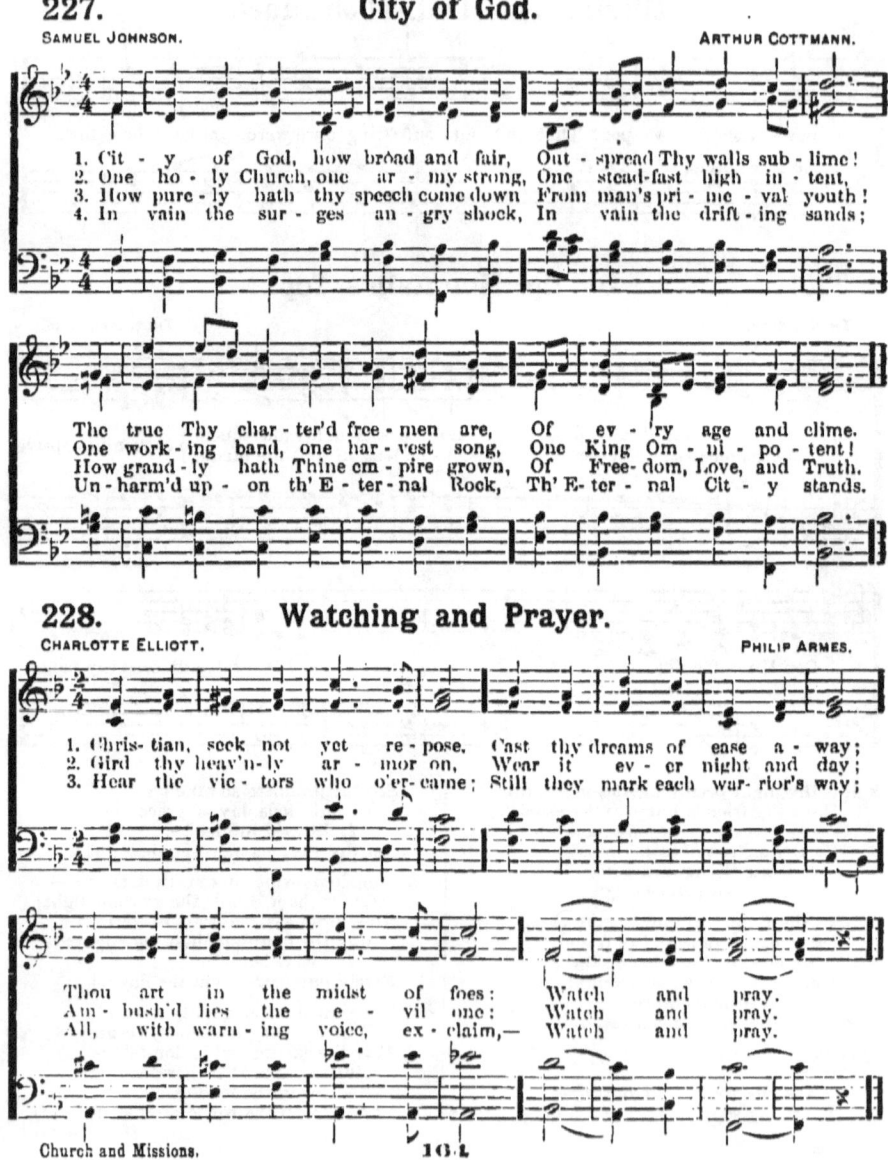

229. Where are Kings and Empires Now?

Rev. A. C. Coxe.   Wm. Croft.

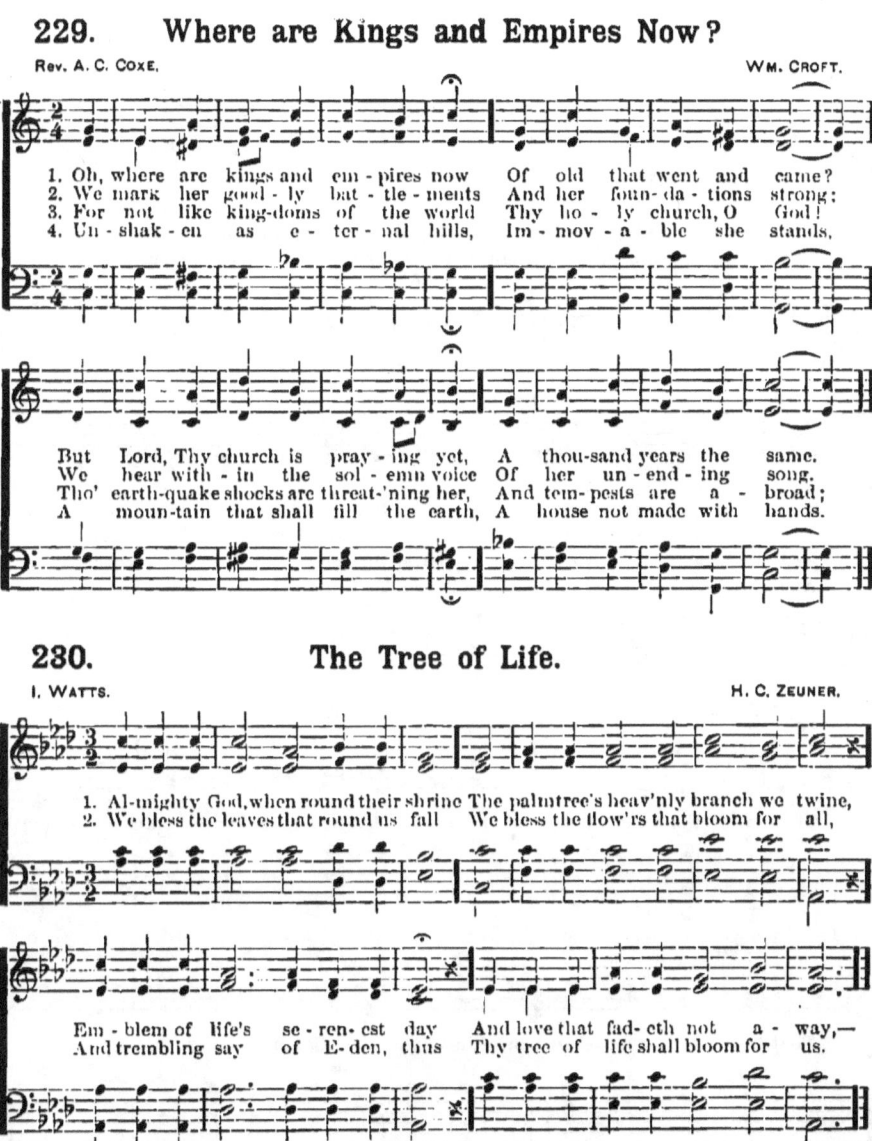

1. Oh, where are kings and em-pires now Of old that went and came?
2. We mark her good-ly bat-tle-ments And her foun-da-tions strong;
3. For not like king-doms of the world Thy ho-ly church, O God!
4. Un-shak-en as e-ter-nal hills, Im-mov-a-ble she stands,

But Lord, Thy church is pray-ing yet, A thou-sand years the same.
We hear with-in the sol-emn voice Of her un-end-ing song.
Tho' earth-quake shocks are threat-'ning her, And tem-pests are a-broad;
A moun-tain that shall fill the earth, A house not made with hands.

230. The Tree of Life.

I. Watts.   H. C. Zeuner.

1. Al-mighty God, when round their shrine The palm-tree's heav'nly branch we twine,
2. We bless the leaves that round us fall We bless the flow'rs that bloom for all,

Em-blem of life's se-ren-est day And love that fad-eth not a-way,—
And trembling say of E-den, thus Thy tree of life shall bloom for us.

Church and Missions.

231. Arise and Sing!

R. WALMSLEY.
JUANITA JONES.

1. A-rise and sing! on Hope's bright wing Send forth the bless-ed sto-ry,
2. The night of wrong has tar-ried long, But see! the day is break-ing;
3. The spread-ing light shall put to flight The things that hurt and grieve us;
4. Ye that are men, with tongue and pen, Speed on the con-sum-ma-tion;

That night shall go, and day shall grow From glo-ry un-to glo-ry.
And at the sign, and touch di-vine, The world from sleep is wak-ing.
And peace and love, from heav'n a-bove, Des-cend and nev-er leave us.
And chil-dren, bring your songs and sing, Of Christ, the world's sal-va-tion.

CHORUS.

Then raise the song, the grand old song, That wrong shall tri-umph nev-er;

That truth and right shall win the fight, Since Christ is King for ev-er.

Triumph.

233. Hail the Cross of Jesus!

Anon.   Sir. A. S. Sullivan.

1. Hail the cross of Je-sus! Lift it up on high! Hail the mighty sig-nal Point-ing to the sky! Hail the guide of pil-grims Thro' each de-sert drear! Hail the sign of Je-sus, Chas-ing far our fear!
2. Stands the cross of Je-sus Foremost in the fight, Drawing ev-er all men By its wondrous might. See! it mov-eth on-ward; Glad-ly fol-low we; Where-so-e'er it go-eth, Should Christ's soldiers be.
3. Crowns and thrones may perish, Kingdoms rise and wane; But the Cross of Je-sus Glo-rious will re-main; At this sign of tri-umph, Sin's dark host doth flee; On, then, Christian sol-diers! On to vic-to-ry!

CHORUS.

Hail the Cross of Je-sus! Lift it up on high! Hail the mighty sig-nal Point-ing to the sky!

234.

1 God's free mercy streameth
  Over all the world.
And His banner gleameth
  Everywhere unfurled.
Broad and deep and glorious
  As the heaven above,
Triumph.

Shines in might victorious
  His eternal Love.
Cho.—God's free mercy streameth
  Over all the world.
And His banner gleameth
  Everywhere unfurled.

2 Lord, upon our blindness,
　Thy pure radiance pour;
　For Thy loving-kindness
　Make us love Thee more.
　And when clouds are drifting
　Dark across our sky,
　Then, the veil uplifting,
　Father, be Thou nigh.—CHO.

3 We will never doubt Thee;
　Though Thou veil Thy light;
　Life is dark without Thee;
　Death with Thee is bright.
　Light of Light! shine o'er us
　On our pilgrim way,
　Go, Thou still before us
　To the endless day.—CHO.

Anon.

235.

1 Jesus is our Pilot,
　No one else can guide
　Our frail barque in safety
　O'er life's stormy tide.
　When the waves of trouble
　Baffle human skill,
　He can always calm them
　With His "Peace, be still."

CHO.—Jesus is our Pilot,
　Guided by His hand,
　We shall reach the haven
　On the golden strand.

2 Jesus is our Pilot,
　Through His mighty arm
　We are safe from danger—
　Safe from fear and harm.
　In His strong protection
　We may ever rest;
　Refuge from all sorrow
　Is His faithful breast.—CHO.

3 Jesus is our Pilot,
　Well He knows the way
　From this realm of shadows
　To the realm of day.
　He can find the harbor
　Others seek in vain,
　There the Lord of glory
　Evermore He'll reign.—CHO.

Kate Cameron.

236. Triumphant Zion.

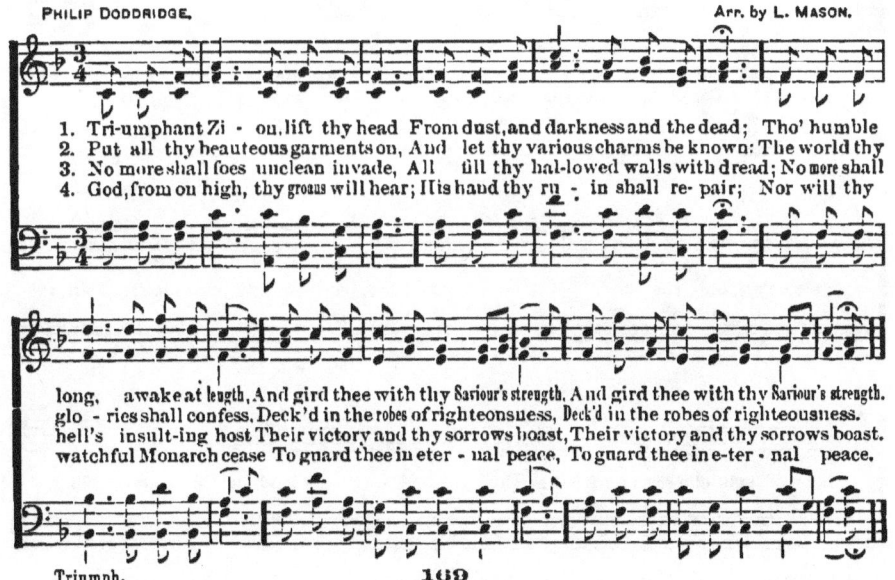

PHILIP DODDRIDGE. Arr. by L. MASON.

1. Tri-umphant Zi - on, lift thy head From dust, and darkness and the dead; Tho' humble
2. Put all thy beauteous garments on, And let thy various charms be known: The world thy
3. No more shall foes unclean invade, All fill thy hal-lowed walls with dread; No more shall
4. God, from on high, thy groans will hear; His hand thy ru - in shall re - pair; Nor will thy

long, awake at length, And gird thee with thy Saviour's strength, And gird thee with thy Saviour's strength.
glo - ries shall confess, Deck'd in the robes of righteousness, Deck'd in the robes of righteousness.
hell's insult-ing host Their victory and thy sorrows boast, Their victory and thy sorrows boast.
watchful Monarch cease To guard thee in eter - nal peace, To guard thee in e-ter - nal peace.

Triumph.

238. O Blessed Lord, I Come.

FANNY J. CROSBY. IRA D. SANKEY.

1. O Jesus, Saviour, hear my call, While at Thy feet I humbly fall;
2. I have no merit of my own, Thou only canst for sin atone;
3. Thy precious name salvation brings, To Thee my weary spirit clings;
4. O take this wand'ring heart of mine, And seal it, Lord, forever Thine;

To Thee, my Hope, my Life, my all, O blessed Lord, I come.
And looking up to Thee alone, O blessed Lord, I come.
And now, to rest beneath Thy wings, O blessed Lord, I come.
That I may know Thy love divine, O blessed Lord, I come.

CHORUS.

I come, and this my only plea, That Thou didst give Thyself for me,
And casting all my care on Thee, O blessed Lord, I come.

Copyright, 1893, by The Biglow & Main Co.

Triumph.

239. The Child of a King!

HATTIE E. BUELL.
JOHN B. SUMNER, arr.

1. My Father is rich in hous-es and lands, He hold-eth the wealth of the world in His hands! Of ru-bies and diamonds, of sil-ver and gold, His cof-fers are full, He has rich-es un-told.
2. My Father's own Son, the Sav-iour of men, Once wan-der'd o'er earth as the poor-est of them; But now He is reigning for ev-er on high, And will give me a home in heav'n by and by.
3. I once was an out-cast stran-ger on earth, A sin-ner by choice, an a-lien by birth! But I've been a-dopt-ed, my name's written down,—And heir to a mansion, a robe, and a crown!
4. A tent or a cot-tage, why should I care? They'r building a pal-ace for me o-ver there! Tho' ex-iled from home, yet still I may sing: All glo-ry to God, I'm the child of a King!

CHORUS.

I'm the child of a King! The child of a King! With Je-sus my Sav-iour, I'm the child of a King!

ad lib.

Triumph

Copyright, 1882, by Biglow & Main.

240. Rolling Onward.

GRACE J. FRANCES.   HUBERT P. MAIN.

1. As the distant streams u-nit-ing, To the o-cean on-ward move,
2. 'Tis the cho-rus of an ar-my Do-ing bat-tle for the Lord,
3. 'Tis the cho-rus of the faith-ful Pressing on to win the prize,
4. May the praise that now is of-fered From this ho-ly place of prayer,

So our songs of joy are blend-ing With the songs of those a-bove.
'Tis the ech-o of the mar-tyrs Who have con-quered thro' His word.
'Tis the an-them of the mill-ions Gathered safe be-yond the skies.
Rise to heav'n, and sweet-ly min-gle With the songs of an-gels there.

CHORUS.

Roll-ing on-ward, sweeping downward, At the gold-en gate they meet:

Songs from earth and songs in glo-ry Break as one, at Je-sus' feet.

Triumph.   Copyright, 1886, by Biglow & Main.

Battle Hymn of the Women's Crusade.—Concluded.

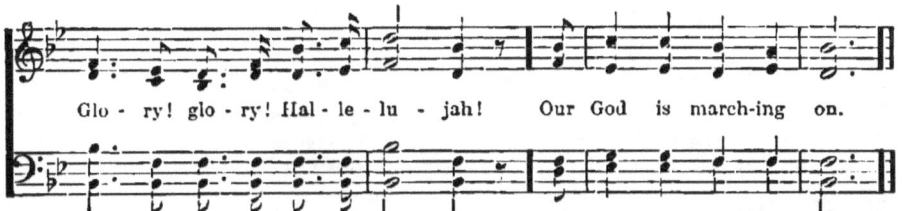

Glo - ry! glo - ry! Hal - le - lu - jah! Our God is march-ing on.

242.

(This poem, by the wife of the president of Amherst College, was written for the eighteenth anniversary of the Massachusetts W. C. T. U.)

1 From the hills and from the valleys,
  Ring a glad, triumphant song;
'Tis the hymn of human progress,
  In its strife divine with wrong;
'Tis the golden, heavenly anthem,
  Which earth's faithful ones prolong,
  "Our Christ is strong to save!"

Cho.—Glory, glory, hallelujah,
  Glory, glory, hallelujah,
  Glory, glory, hallelujah,
  Our Christ is strong to save!

2 He who died in pain and sorrow,
  That His people might be free;
He who, conquering death, and rising,
  Captive led captivity,—
He our glorious, living Leader,
  Calls us on to victory—
  "For Christ is strong to save!"—Cho.

3 He will bid the powers of evil
  Crumble to their final fall;
He will raise the bruised and broken,
  And set free each prisoned thrall;
Who is he that may not conquer
  Since his Lord has conquered all?"
  "And Christ is strong to save!"—Cho.

4 O the growing, widening wonder
  Of the gospel of His grace!
In His world-encircling service,
  Every worker finds a place.

For we only turn dark natures
  Toward the brightness of His face;
  "And Christ is strong to save!"—Cho.

5 Onward sweeps the gathering army
  Luminous in living light,
Forward stream the hallowed banners,
  Floating far their snowy white,
Upward swells the mighty war cry
  Still, "for God and Home and Right!
  "Our Christ is strong to save!"—Cho.
  Mrs. Merrill E. Gates.

243.   Tune—AMERICA. (Page 177.)

1 God bless the noble band,
  Who work to save our land
    From drink and shame:
  And labor to bring in
  Men from paths of sin,
  A new life to begin
    In Jesus' name.

2 Thus homes are bright once more;
  As in the days of yore,
    True love reigns there:
  Hushed is the cruel word,
  With joy each heart is stirred,
  The voice of praise is heard
    Filling the air.

3 God bless each noble band,
  In this and every land,
    Who work for Thee,—
  The drunkard to restore
  That he may sin no more,
  But Thy name, Lord, adore,
    Eternally.
      Wm. James.

Temperance.

244. The Temperance Call.

Mrs. C. G. Goodwin. Franz Abt.

1. Hear the temp'rance call, Freemen, one and all! Hear your country's earnest cry; See your na-tive land Lift its beck'ning hand. "Sons of freedom, come ye nigh, come ye nigh;
2. Leave the shop and farm; Leave your bright hearths warm; To the polls! the land to save; Let your lead-ers be True and no-ble, free, Fearless temp'rate, good, and brave, good and brave;
3. Hail, our fa-ther-land! Here Thy children stand, All resolved, u-nit-ed, true, In the temp'rance cause Ne'er to faint or pause; This our pur-pose is, and vow; this our vow,

CHORUS.
Chase the mon-ster from our shore; Let his cru-el reign be o'er. Chase the mon-ster from our shore; Let his cru-el reign be o'er.

By per. The Bigelow & Main Co.

Temperance.

248. Praise the Lord of Harvest.

J. HAMILTON.   E. PROUT.

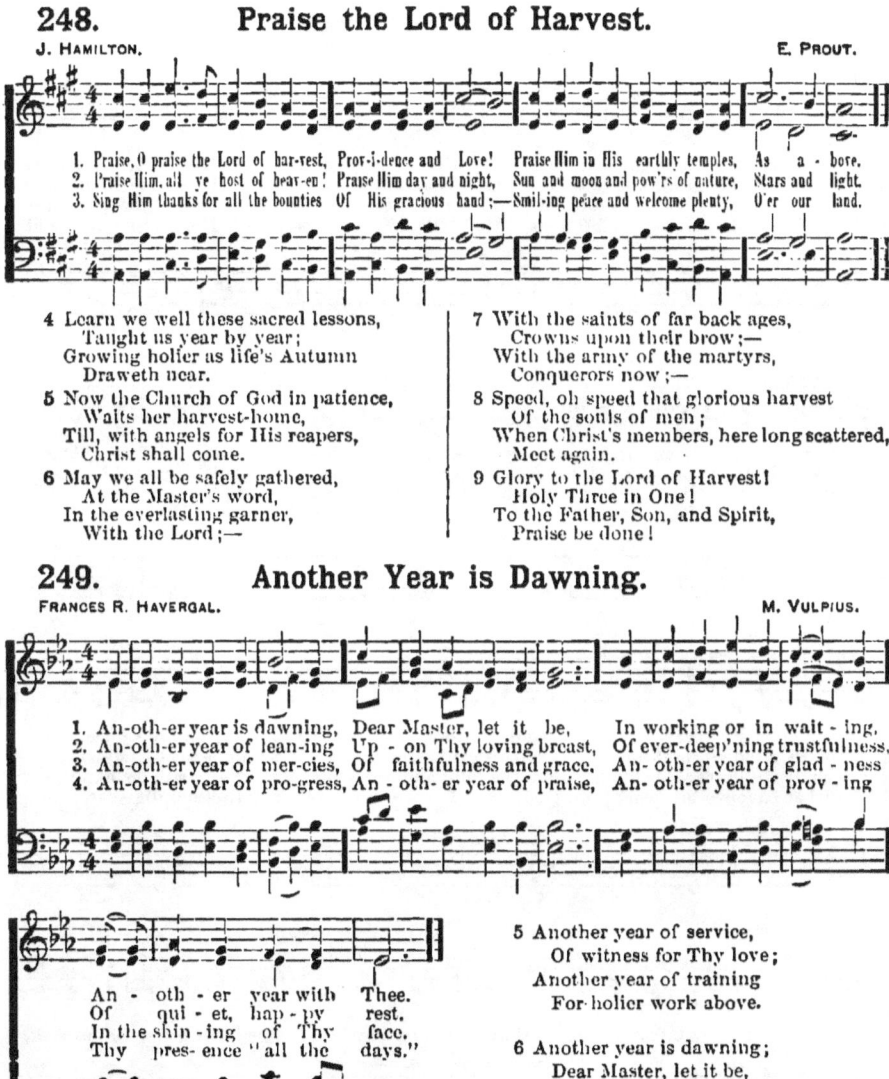

1. Praise, O praise the Lord of har-vest, Prov-i-dence and Love! Praise Him in His earthly temples, As a - bove.
2. Praise Him, all ye host of heav-en! Praise Him day and night, Sun and moon and pow'rs of nature, Stars and light.
3. Sing Him thanks for all the bounties Of His gracious hand;— Smil-ing peace and welcome plenty, O'er our land.

4 Learn we well these sacred lessons,
  Taught us year by year;
Growing holier as life's Autumn
  Draweth near.

5 Now the Church of God in patience,
  Waits her harvest-home,
Till, with angels for His reapers,
  Christ shall come.

6 May we all be safely gathered,
  At the Master's word,
In the everlasting garner,
  With the Lord;—

7 With the saints of far back ages,
  Crowns upon their brow;—
With the army of the martyrs,
  Conquerors now;—

8 Speed, oh speed that glorious harvest
  Of the souls of men;
When Christ's members, here long scattered,
  Meet again.

9 Glory to the Lord of Harvest!
  Holy Three in One!
To the Father, Son, and Spirit,
  Praise be done!

249. Another Year is Dawning.

FRANCES R. HAVERGAL.   M. VULPIUS.

1. An-oth-er year is dawning, Dear Master, let it be, In working or in wait - ing,
2. An-oth-er year of lean-ing Up - on Thy loving breast, Of ever-deep'ning trustfulness,
3. An-oth-er year of mer-cies, Of faithfulness and grace, An- oth-er year of glad - ness
4. An-oth-er year of pro-gress, An - oth- er year of praise, An- oth-er year of prov - ing

An - oth - er year with Thee.
Of qui - et, hap - py rest.
In the shin - ing of Thy face.
Thy pres- ence "all the days."

5 Another year of service,
  Of witness for Thy love;
Another year of training
  For holier work above.

6 Another year is dawning;
  Dear Master, let it be,
On earth, or else in heaven,
  Another year for Thee!

Times and Seasons.

250. The Opening Year.

FRANCES R. HAVERGAL.   French Air.

1. Stand-ing at the por-tal of the op-'ning year, Words of com-fort meet us, hush-ing ev-'ry fear; Spo-ken thro' the si-lence by our Fa-ther's voice. Ten-der, strong, and faithful, mak-ing us re-joice.
2. I, the Lord, am with thee, be thou not a-fraid, I will help and strength-en, be thou not dis-may'd! Yea, I will up-hold thee with My own right hand. Thou art call'd and cho-sen in My sight to stand.
3. For the year be-fore us, oh, what rich sup-plies! For the poor and need-y liv-ing streams shall rise; For the sad and sin-ful shall His grace a-bound; For the faint and fee-ble per-fect strength be found.
4. He will nev-er fail us, He will not for-sake; His e-ter-nal cov-'nant He will nev-er break. Rest-ing on His prom-ise, what have we to fear? God is all suf-fi-cient for the com-ing year.

ff CHORUS.

On-ward then and fear not, chil-dren of the day! For His word shall nev-er,

Times and Seasons.

The Opening Year.—Concluded.

nev-er pass a-way! For His word shall nev-er, nev-er pass a-way!

251.   **Thanks to God.**

GRACE J. FRANCES.   HUBERT P. MAIN.

1. Thanks to God whose hand has led us Thro' an-oth-er hap-py year;
2. Thanks for birds that sweet-ly car - ol, On their light and air - y wing;
3. Thanks to Him, our great Cre - a - tor, For the joy the sum-mer yields;

Thanks to God whose ten - der mer - cy Kept us safe and brought us here.
For the clouds that float a - bove us, And the gen - tle rain they bring.
Fruits that prom - ise full and plen - ty, In the gold - en har - vest fields.

D.S.—*Yet, for homes and friends that love us, We would thank Him most of all.*

CHORUS.

Thanks for these and all the bless-ings From His grac-ious hand that fall;

Copyright, 1888, by Biglow & Main.

Times and Seasons.

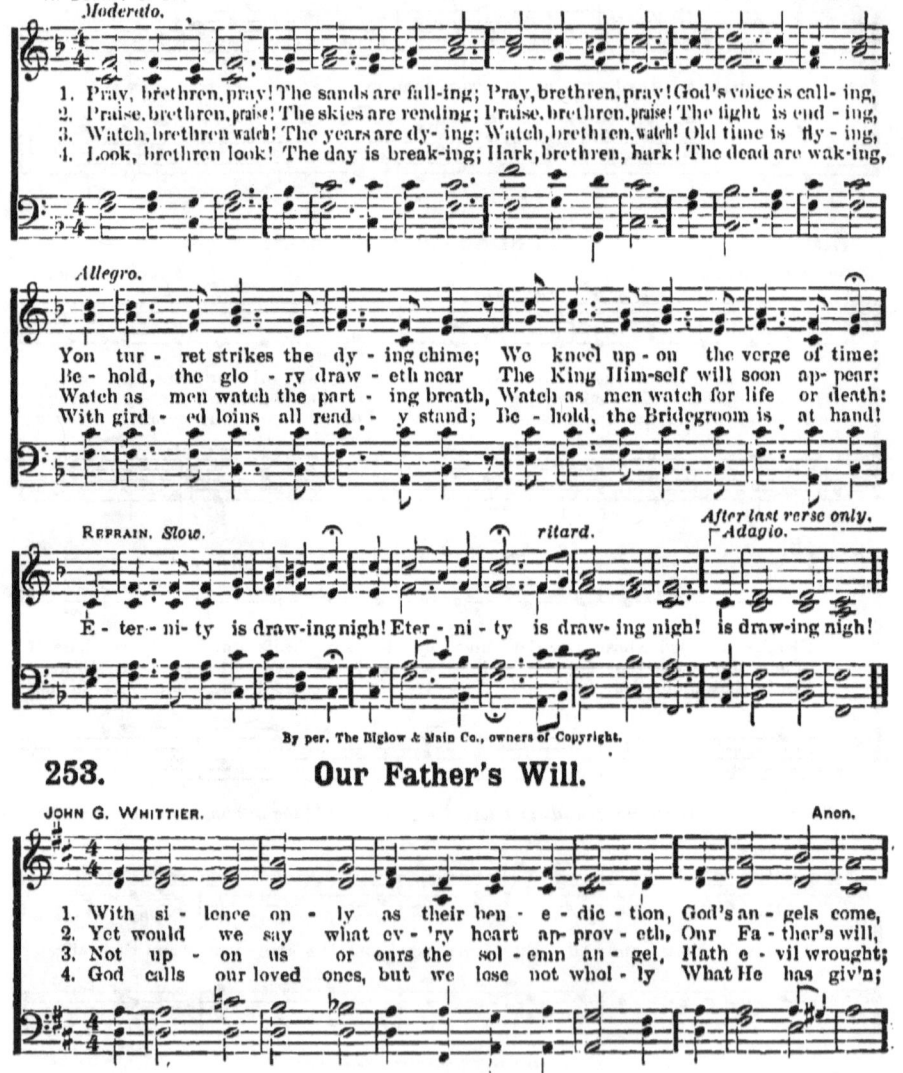

Our Father's Will.—Concluded.

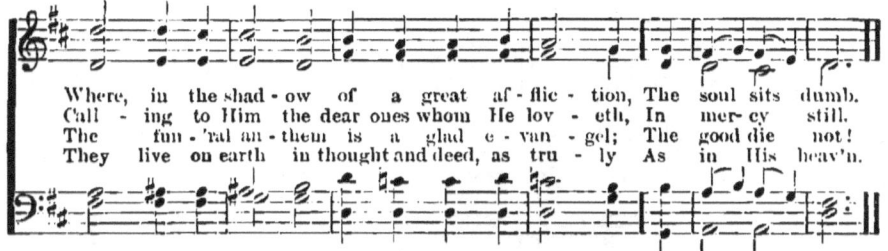

Where, in the shad-ow of a great af-flic-tion, The soul sits dumb.
Call-ing to Him the dear ones whom He lov-eth, In mer-cy still.
The fun-'ral an-them is a glad e-van-gel; The good die not!
They live on earth in thought and deed, as tru-ly As in His heav'n.

254. In the Hour of Trial.

JAMES MONTGOMERY. SPENCER LANE.

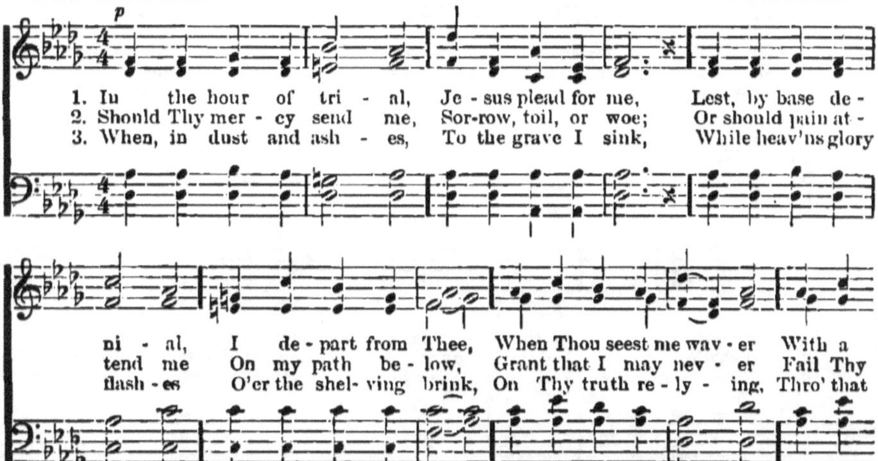

1. In the hour of tri-al, Jesus plead for me, Lest, by base de-ni-al, I de-part from Thee, When Thou seest me wav-er With a look re-call;.. Nor for fear or fa-vor, Suf-fer me to fall.
2. Should Thy mer-cy send me, Sor-row, toil, or woe; Or should pain at-tend me On my path be-low, Grant that I may nev-er Fail Thy hand to see,.. Grant that I may ev-er, Cast my care on Thee.
3. When, in dust and ash-es, To the grave I sink, While heav'ns glory flash-es O'er the shel-ving brink, On Thy truth re-ly-ing, Thro' that mor-tal strife,. Lord, re-ceive me, dy-ing, To e-ter-nal life.

Used by permission from "Hutchins' Hymnal."

Affliction.

255. When Twilight Gathers Fast.

Anon.   Rev. O. R. Barnicott.

1. When the twi-light gath-ers fast, With a qui-et still and deep, When the bus-y day has passed, And the wea-ry "falls on sleep;" When the life-long toil is o'er, At the set-ting of the sun, Comes joy for-ev-er more, With the Mas-ter's word, "Well done!" With the Mas-ter's word, "Well done!"

2. 'Mid the tread of ma-ny feet, 'Mid the hur-ry and the throng, In the bur-den and the heat, Have the work-ing hours seemed long? Soft-ly the shadow falls, And the pil-grim's race is run; While thro' ce-les-tial halls, Re-sounds the glad "Well done!" Re-sounds the glad "Well done!"

3. Well worth the dai-ly cross; Well worth the earn-est toil; Well worth re-proach and loss, The fight on stran-ger soil! Let us lift our hearts and pray, And take our jour-ney on; Work while 'tis called to-day, With the tho't of that "Well done!" With the tho't of that "Well done!"

Affliction.

256. Tenting by the Shore.

Rev. W. O. Cushing.
Rev. Robert Lowry.

1. Tent-ing by the shore of the great, deep sea, Wait-ing on the wave-worn strand,
2. Hap-py now with Je-sus, they want no more, Knowing neith-er pain nor care;
3. Tent-ing by the shore of the great, deep sea, Rest-ing in the Lord, I wait;

Ten-der are the voic - es call-ing un - to me, Voic - es from the si - lent land.
Still they seem to lin - ger, waiting on the shore, Point-ing to the glo - ry there.
Still the lov - ing voic - es sweet-ly call to me, Float-ing from the gold - en gate.

CHORUS.

They are not dead, they are not dead, They have only pass'd the cold, dark river; We shall meet them once again, Yes, we'll meet them once a-gain, With Je-sus, in our home for ev - er.

Affliction.

Copyright, 1881, by Biglow & Main.

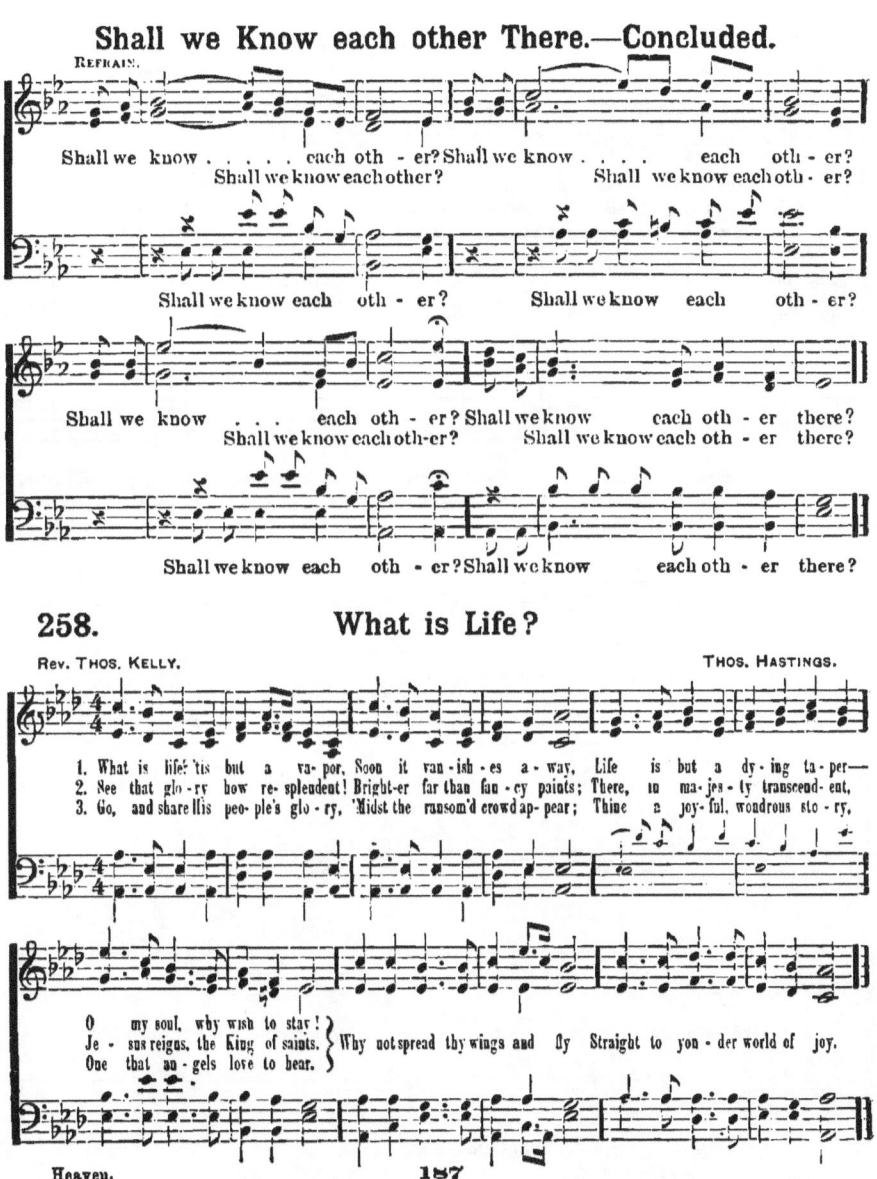

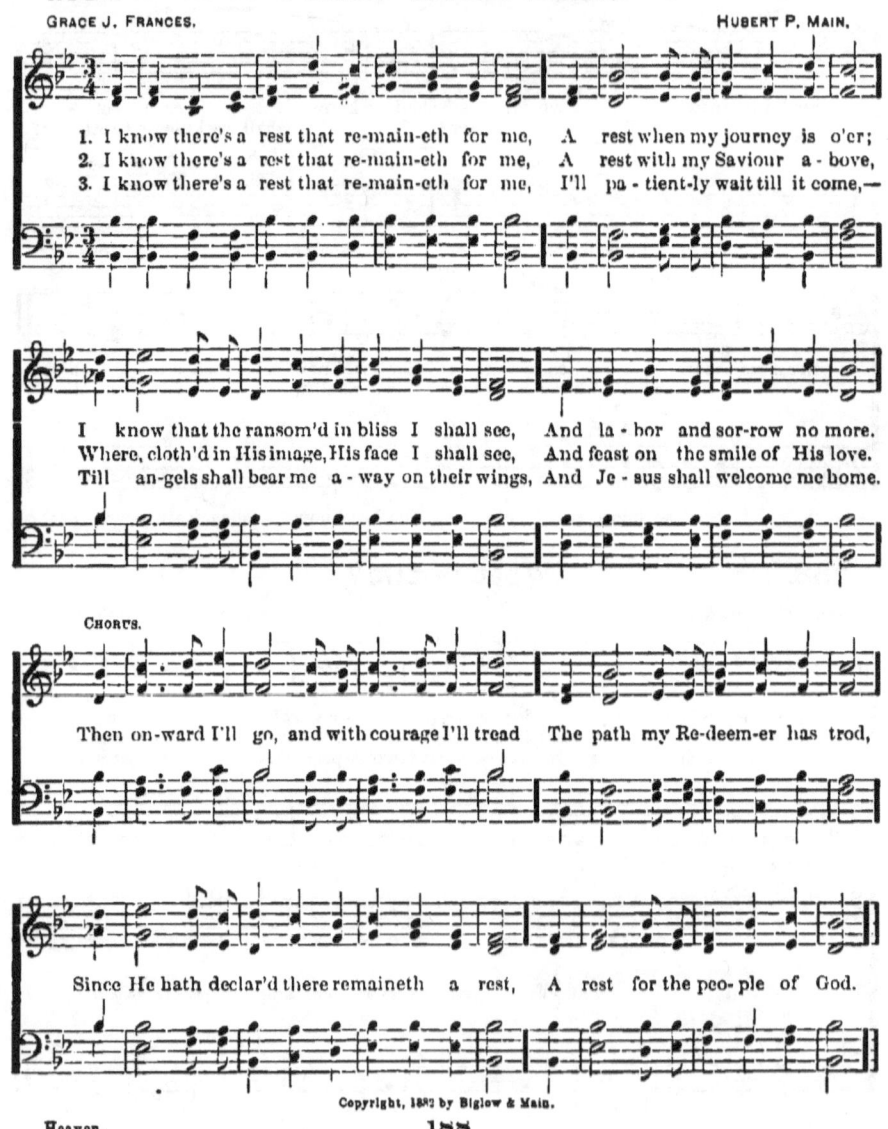

261. Love, Rest, and Home!

H. BONAR, D. D.
WM. B. BRADBURY.

1. Be-yond the smil-ing and the weep-ing, I shall be soon; Be-yond the waking and the sleeping, Be-yond the sowing and the reaping, I shall be soon.
2. Be-yond the ris-ing and the set-ting, I shall be soon; Be-yond the calming and the fret-ting, Be-yond remembering, for-get-ting, I shall be soon.
3. Be-yond the part-ing and the meet-ing, I shall be soon; Be-yond the farewell and the greeting, Be-yond the pulse's fever beat-ing, I shall be soon.
4. Be-yond the frost-chain and the fe-ver, I shall be soon; Be-yond the rock-waste and the river, Be-yond the ev-er and the nev-er, I shall be soon.

Love, rest, and home! Sweet, sweet home! O how sweet it will be there to meet The dear ones all at home. O how sweet it will be there to meet The dear ones all at home.

Copyright, 1865, by Wm. B. Bradbury.

Heaven.

262. Blessed Home-Land.

GRACE J. FRANCES.   HUBERT P. MAIN.

1. Glid-ing o'er life's fit-ful wa-ters, Heav-y surg-es some-times roll;
2. Oft we catch a faint re-flec-tion Of its bright and ver-nal hills;
3. To our Fa-ther, and our Sav-iour, To the Spir-it, Three in One,
4. 'Tis the wea-ry pil-grim's Home-land, Where each throbbing care shall cease,

And we sigh for yon-der ha-ven, For the Home-land of the soul.
And, tho' dis-tant, how we hail it! How each heart with rapt-ure thrills!
We shall sing glad songs of tri-umph When our har-vest work is done.
And our long-ings and our yearn-ings, Like a wave, be hushed to peace.

REFRAIN.

Bless-ed Home-land, ev-er fair! Sin can nev-er en-ter there;
But the soul, to life a-wak-ing, Ev-er-last-ing bloom shall wear.

Copyright, 1877, by Biglow & Main.

Heaven.

Not Half has ever been Told.—Concluded.

264. Looking Homeward.

GODFREY THRING.   LOWELL MASON.

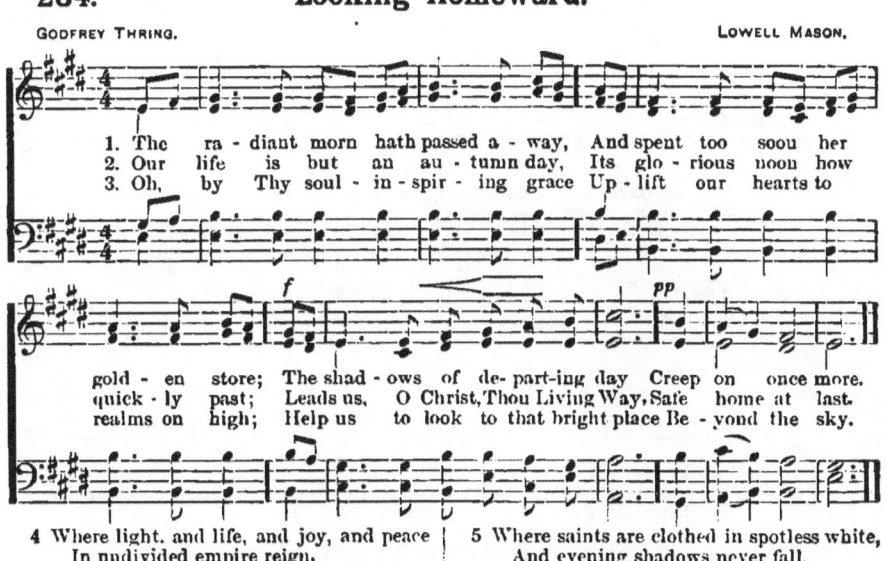

1. The radiant morn hath passed away, And spent too soon her golden store; The shadows of departing day Creep on once more.
2. Our life is but an autumn day, Its glorious noon how quickly past; Leads us, O Christ, Thou Living Way, Safe home at last.
3. Oh, by Thy soul-inspiring grace Uplift our hearts to realms on high; Help us to look to that bright place Beyond the sky.

4 Where light, and life, and joy, and peace
In undivided empire reign,
And thronging angels never cease
Their deathless strain.

5 Where saints are clothed in spotless white,
And evening shadows never fall,
Where Thou Eternal Light of Light,
Art Lord of all.

Heaven.

265. The Bright Forever.

FANNY J. CROSBY. HUBERT P. MAIN.

1. Break-ing thro' the clouds that gath-er O'er the Christian's na-tal skies, Dis-tant beams, like floods of glo - ry, Fill the soul with glad surprise; And we al-most hear the ech - o Of the pure and ho-ly throng, In the bright, the bright for-ev-er, In the sum - mer - land of song.

2. Yet a lit - tle while we lin - ger, Ere we reach our jour-ney's end; Yet a lit - tle while of la - bor, Ere the evening shades descend; Then we'll lay us down to slumber, But the night will soon be o'er; In the bright, the bright for-ev-er, We shall slum - ber nev - er-more.

3. O the bliss of life e - ter - nal! O the long un-brok-en rest! In the gold - en fields of pleasure, In the re-gion of the blest; But, to see our dear Re-deemer, And be-fore His throne to fall, There to hear His gracious welcome— Will be sweet - er far than all.

Chorus.

On the banks be-yond the riv - er, We shall meet, no more to

Heaven.   Copyright, 1871, by Biglow & Main.

The Bright Forever.—Concluded.

sev - er; In the bright, the bright for - ev - er, In the sum-mer-land of song.

266. Beautiful Hills of Glory.

GRACE J. FRANCES.   HUBERT P. MAIN.

1. Beau-ti-ful hills of glo - ry, Beau-ti-ful fields of light, When shall my long-ing
2. Beau-ti-ful strains whose ech-o Oft in my soul I hear, Songs from the ma-ny
3. Not till the voice of Je - sus Tells me my work is done; Not till the race be

REFRAIN.

spir - it Bathe in their splendor bright? When will my loving Sav - iour Call me a-
man-sions, Fall on my list-'ning ear. When will, etc.
end - ed, Not till the crown be won. Then will my lov-ing Sav - iour Call me a-

cross the sea? Beau-ti-ful home e - ter - nal, When shall I come to thee?
cross the sea; Beau-ti-ful home e - ter - nal, Then will I come to thee.

Copyright, 1894, by Biglow & Main.

Heaven.

269. Beautiful Land of Rest.

R. LOWRY.
Rev. R. LOWRY. Arr.

1. Je - ru - sa - lem, for ev - er bright, Beautiful land of rest! No win-ter there nor
2. Je - ru - sa - lem, for ev - er free, Beautiful land of rest! The soul's sweet home of
3. Je - ru - sa - lem, for ev - er dear, Beautiful land of rest! Thy pearly gates al -

chill of night, Beau-ti-ful land of rest! The dripping cloud is chas'd away, The
lib - er - ty, Beau-ti-ful land of rest! The gyves of sin, the chains of woe, The
most ap-pear, Beau-ti-ful land of rest! And when we tread thy lovely shore, We'll

sun breaks forth in end-less day. Je - ru - sa - lem, Je - ru - sa - lem, The beau-ti-ful
ransom'd there will never know, Je - ru - sa - lem, Je - ru - sa - lem, The beau-ti-ful
sing the song we've sung before, Je - ru - sa - lem, Je - ru - sa - lem, The beau-ti-ful

CHORUS.

land of rest!
land of rest! } Beau-ti-ful land! Beau-ti-ful land! Beau-ti-ful land of rest!
land of rest!

Heaven.

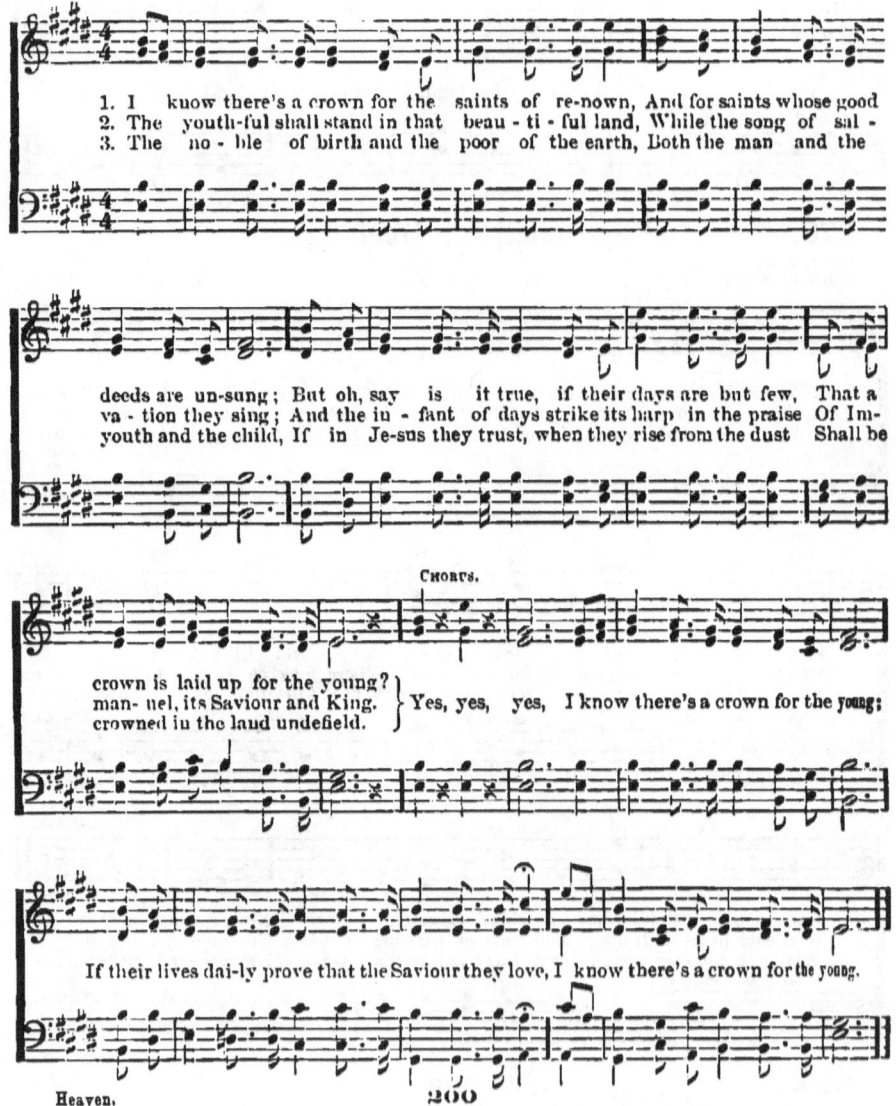

272. Nothing but Leaves!

Mrs. L. E. Akerman. Silas J. Vail.

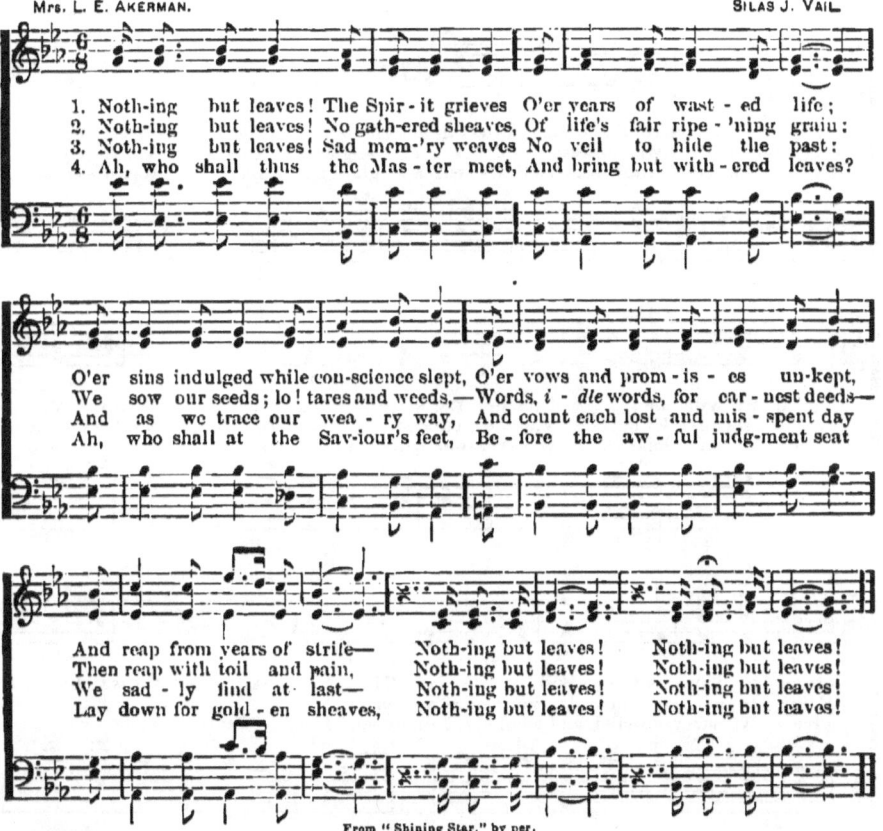

1. Nothing but leaves! The Spirit grieves O'er years of wasted life;
O'er sins indulged while conscience slept, O'er vows and promises unkept,
And reap from years of strife— Nothing but leaves! Nothing but leaves!

2. Nothing but leaves! No gathered sheaves, Of life's fair ripening grain:
We sow our seeds; lo! tares and weeds,—Words, idle words, for earnest deeds—
Then reap with toil and pain, Nothing but leaves! Nothing but leaves!

3. Nothing but leaves! Sad mem'ry weaves No veil to hide the past:
And as we trace our weary way, And count each lost and misspent day,
We sadly find at last— Nothing but leaves! Nothing but leaves!

4. Ah, who shall thus the Master meet, And bring but withered leaves?
Ah, who shall at the Saviour's feet, Before the awful judgment seat
Lay down for golden sheaves, Nothing but leaves! Nothing but leaves!

From "Shining Star," by per.

273 Tune.—WONDROUS LOVE.

1 God loved the world of sinners lost
  And ruined by the fall;
Salvation full, at highest cost,
  He offers free to all.

Cho.—Oh, 'twas love, 'twas wondrous love!
  The love of God to me;
It brought my Saviour from above,
  To die on Calvary.

2 E'en now by faith I claim Him mine,
  The risen Son of God;
Redemption by His death I find,
  And cleansing through the blood.

3 Love brings the glorious fullness in,
  And to His saints makes known
The blessed rest from inbred sin,
  Through faith in Christ alone.

Martha M. Stockton.

274. True Hearted, Whole Hearted.

FRANCES R. HAVERGAL. GEO. C. STEBBINS, by per.

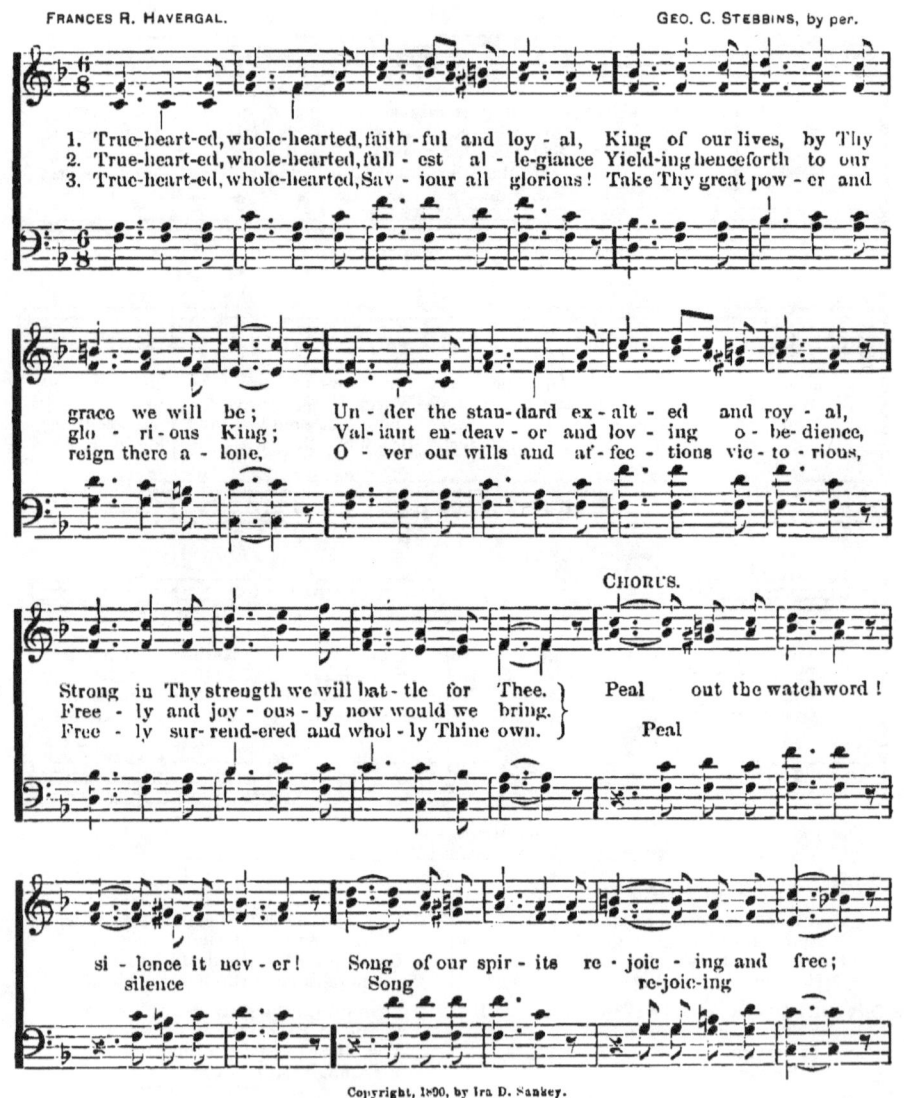

1. True-heart-ed, whole-hearted, faith-ful and loy-al, King of our lives, by Thy grace we will be; Un-der the stau-dard ex-alt-ed and roy-al, Strong in Thy strength we will bat-tle for Thee.
2. True-heart-ed, whole-hearted, full-est al-le-giance Yield-ing henceforth to our glo-ri-ous King; Val-iant en-deav-or and lov-ing o-be-dience, Free-ly and joy-ous-ly now would we bring.
3. True-heart-ed, whole-hearted, Sav-iour all glorious! Take Thy great pow-er and reign there a-lone, O-ver our wills and af-fec-tions vic-to-rious, Free-ly sur-rend-ered and whol-ly Thine own.

CHORUS.

Peal out the watchword! si-lence it nev-er! Song of our spir-its re-joic-ing and free;

Copyright, 1890, by Ira D. Sankey.

Miscellaneous.

True Hearted, Whole Hearted.—Concluded.

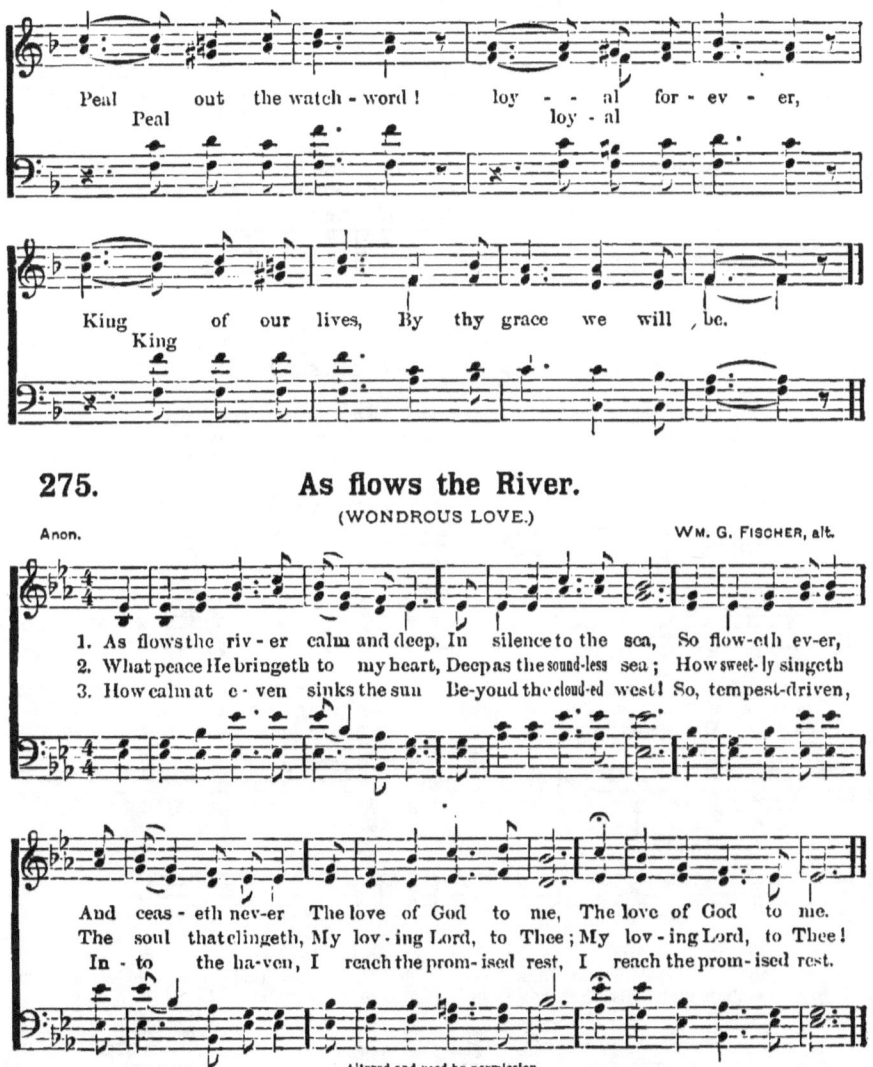

Peal out the watch-word! loy - - al for - ev - er,
Peal loy - al
King of our lives, By thy grace we will be.
King

275. **As flows the River.**
(WONDROUS LOVE.)

Anon. WM. G. FISCHER, alt.

1. As flows the riv-er calm and deep, In silence to the sea, So flow-eth ev-er,
2. What peace He bringeth to my heart, Deep as the sound-less sea; How sweet-ly singeth
3. How calm at e-ven sinks the sun Be-yond the cloud-ed west! So, tempest-driven,

And ceas-eth nev-er The love of God to me, The love of God to me.
The soul that clingeth, My lov-ing Lord, to Thee; My lov-ing Lord, to Thee!
In - to the ha-ven, I reach the prom-ised rest, I reach the prom-ised rest.

Altered and used by permission.

Miscellaneous.

Master, the Tempest is Raging.—Concluded.

277. **Lord Dismiss Us.**

JOHN FAWCETT. WM. L. VINER.

1. Lord, dis-miss us with Thy bless-ing, Fill our hearts with joy and peace;
2. Thanks we give, and a-dor-a-tion, For Thy gos-pel's joy-ful sound;
3. So, when-e'er the sig-nal's giv-en Us from earth to call a-way,

Let us each, Thy love pos-sess-ing, Tri-umph in re-deem-ing grace;
May the fruits of Thy sal-va-tion, In our hearts and lives a-bound;
Borne on an-gels' wings to heav-en, Glad the sum-mons to o-bey,

O re-fresh us, O re-fresh us, Trav-'ling through this wil-der-ness.
May Thy pres-ence May Thy pres-ence, With us ev-er-more be found.
May we ev-er May we ev-er, Reign with Christ in end-less day.

*The Repeat for following Hymns.

278.
May the grace of Christ our Saviour,
  And the Father's boundless love,
With the Holy Spirit's favor,
  Rest upon us from above:
Thus may we abide in union
  With each other and the Lord;
And possess, in sweet communion,
  Joys which earth cannot afford.
            John Newton.

Dismission.

279.
Lord, dismiss us with Thy blessing,
  Bid us now depart in peace;
Still on heavenly manna feeding,
  Let our faith and love increase;
Fill each breast with consolation;
  Up to Thee our hearts we raise:
When we reach our blissful station,
  Then we'll give Thee nobler praise.
            Edwin Smythe.

FAMILIAR HYMNS.

280. THE OLD, OLD STORY.
7. 6.

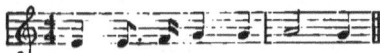

1 Tell me the old, old story
  Of unseen things above,
Of Jesus and His glory,
  Of Jesus and His love.
Tell me the story simply,
  As to a little child,
For I am weak and weary,
  And helpless and defiled.

Ref.—Tell me the old, old story,
  Tell me the old, old story,
  Tell me the old, old story,
  Of Jesus and His love.

2 Tell me the story slowly,
  That I may take it in—
That wonderful redemption,
  God's remedy for sin.
Tell me the story often,
  For I forget so soon!
The "early dew" of morning
  Has passed away at noon.
Kate Hankey.

281. OLIVET. 6. 4.

1 My faith looks up to Thee
  Thou Lamb of Calvary,
    Saviour divine!
  Now hear me while I pray,
  Take all my guilt away,
  Oh! let me from this day,
    Be wholly Thine!

2 May Thy rich grace impart
  Strength to my failing heart;
    My zeal inspire;
  As Thou hast died for me,
  Oh! may my love to Thee
  Pure, warm, and changeless be,
    A living fire!

3 While life's dark maze I tread,
  And griefs around me spread,
    Be Thou my Guide;
  Bid darkness turn to day,
  Wipe sorrow's tears away,
  Nor let me ever stray
    From Thee aside.
Ray Palmer.

282. I LOVE TO TELL THE STORY.
7. 6.

1 I love to tell the story
  Of unseen things above,
Of Jesus and His glory,
  Of Jesus and His love.
I love to tell the story,
  Because I know it's true;
It satisfies my longings,
  As nothing else can do.

Cho.—I love to tell the story,
  'Twill be my theme in glory,
  To tell the old, old story,
  Of Jesus and His love.

2 I love to tell the story,
  More wonderful it seems
Than all the golden fancies
  Of all our golden dreams.
I love to tell the story,
  It did so much for me,
And that is just the reason
  I tell it now to thee.

3 I love to tell the story:
  For those who know it best
Seem hungering and thirsting
  To hear it like the rest.
And when, in scenes of glory,
  I sing the New, New Song,
'Twill be the old, old story
  That I have loved so long!
Kate Hankey.

283. HAPPY DAY. L. M.

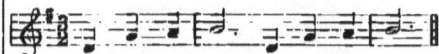

1 O happy day, that fixed my choice
  On Thee, my Saviour and my God!
Well may this glowing heart rejoice
  And tell its raptures all abroad.

Cho.—Happy day, happy day,
  When Jesus washed my sins away;
He taught me how to watch and pray,
  And live rejoicing every day;
Happy day, happy day,
  When Jesus washed my sins away.

2 Now rest, my long-divided heart;
  Fixed on this blissful centre, rest;
Nor ever from Thy Lord depart,
  With Him of every good possessed.
P. Doddridge.

Familiar Hymns.

284. JERUSALEM, THE GOLDEN.

286. I HEARD THE VOICE. C. M.

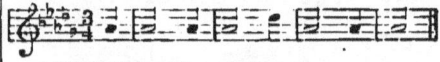

1 Jerusalem the golden,
   With milk and honey blest,
Beneath thy contemplation
   Sink heart and voice to rest.
I know not—oh! I know not
   What joys await me there,
What radiancy of glory,
   What bliss beyond compare.

2 They stand, those halls of Zion,
   All jubilant with song,
And bright with many an angel,
   And all the martyr throng.
There is the throne of David,
   And there, from toil released,
The shout of them that triumph,
   The song of them that feast.

3 Oh, sweet and blessèd country,
   The home of God's elect;
Oh, sweet and blessèd country,
   That eager hearts expect!
Jesus, in mercy bring us
   To that dear land of rest,
Who art, with God the Father
   And Spirit, ever blest.
                      John M. Neale.

1 I heard the voice of Jesus say,
   "Come unto me and rest;
Lay down, thou weary one, lay down
   Thy head upon my breast;"
I came to Jesus as I was,
   Weary, and worn, and sad;
I found in Him a resting-place,
   And He has made me glad.

2 I heard the voice of Jesus say,
   "Behold, I freely give
The living-water! thirsty one,
   Stoop down, and drink, and live.'
I came to Jesus, and I drank
   Of that life-giving stream :
My thirst was quenched, my soul revived,
   And now I live in Him.

3 I heard the voice of Jesus say,
   "I am this dark world's light:
Look unto me; thy morn shall rise,
   And all thy day be bright."
I looked to Jesus and I found
   In Him my Star, my Sun;
And in that light of life I'll walk
   Till all my journey's done.
                      Horatius Bonar.

285. TOPLADY. 7.

287. PILOT. 7.

1 Rock of Ages, cleft for me,
   Let me hide myself in Thee :
Let the water and the blood,
From Thy riven side which flow'd,
Be of sin the double cure,
Save me from its guilt and power.

2 Could my zeal no respite know,
   Could my tears forever flow,
All for sin could not atone;
Thou must save, and Thou alone.
Nothing in my hand I bring,
Simply to Thy cross I cling;

3 While I draw this fleeting breath,
   When my eyelids close in death,
When I soar to worlds unknow,
See thee on Thy judgment throne,—
Rock of Ages! cleft for me,
Let me hide myself in Thee!
                      A. M. Toplady.

1 Jesus, Saviour, pilot me,
   Over life's tempestuous sea;
Unknown waves before me roll,
Hiding rock and treacherous shoal;
Chart and compass come from Thee:
Jesus, Saviour, pilot me.

2 As a mother stills her child,
   Thou canst hush the ocean wild;
Boisterous waves obey Thy will
When Thou say'st to them "Be still!"
Wondrous Sovereign of the sea,
Jesus, Saviour, pilot me.

3 When at last I near the shore,
   And the fearful breakers roar
'Twixt me and the peaceful rest,
Then, while leaning on Thy breast,
May I hear Thee say to me,
"Fear not, I will pilot thee!"
                      Edward Hopper.

Familiar Hymns.

288. WEBB. 7. 6.

1 The morning light is breaking;
  The darkness disappears;
  The sons of earth are waking
  To penitential tears.
  Each breeze that sweeps the ocean
  Brings tidings from afar
  Of nations in commotion,
  Prepared for Zion's war.

2 Rich dews of grace come o'er us
  In many a gentle shower,
  And brighter scenes before us
  Are opening every hour;
  Each cry to heaven going
  Abundant answers brings,
  And heavenly gales are blowing
  With peace upon their wings.

3 Blest river of salvation!
  Pursue thine onward way;
  Flow thou to every nation,
  Nor in thy richness stay—
  Stay not till all the lowly
  Triumphant reach their home;
  Stay not till all the holy
  Proclaim "The Lord is come."
                        S. F. Smith.

289. LABAN. S. M.

1 My soul, be on thy guard,
  Ten thousand foes arise,
  And hosts of sin are pressing hard
  To draw thee from the skies.

2 Oh, watch, and fight, and pray,
  The battle ne'er give o'er,
  Renew it boldly every day,
  And help divine implore.

3 Ne'er think the victory won,
  Nor once at ease sit down;
  Thine arduous work will not be done
  Till thou hast got the crown.

4 Fight on, my soul, till death
  Shall bring thee to thy God:
  He'll take thee, at thy parting breath,
  Up to His blest abode.
                        George Heath.

290. MISSIONARY HYMN. 7. 6.

1 From Greenland's icy mountains,
  From India's coral strand,
  Where Afric's sunny fountains
  Roll down their golden sand,—
  From many an ancient river,
  From many a palmy plain,
  They call us to deliver
  Their land from error's chain.

2 Shall we, whose souls are lighted
  With wisdom from on high,—
  Shall we, to men benighted,
  The Lamp of Life deny?
  Salvation, oh, salvation!
  The joyful sound proclaim,
  Till earth's remotest nation
  Has learned Messiah's name.

3 Waft, waft, ye winds, His story,
  And you, ye waters, roll,
  Till, like a sea of glory,
  It spreads from pole to pole;
  Till o'er our ransomed nature,
  The Lamb for sinners slain,
  Redeemer, King, Creator,
  In bliss returns to reign.
                        R. Heber.

291. EVERY DAY AND HOUR.
           Slowly.

1 Saviour, more than life to me,
  I am clinging, clinging close to Thee;
  Let Thy precious blood applied,
  Keep me ever, ever near Thy side.

REF.—Every day, every hour,
  Let me feel Thy cleansing power:
  May Thy tender love to me,
  Bind me closer, closer, Lord, to **Thee.**

2 Through this changing world below,
  Lead me gently, gently as I go;
  Trusting Thee, I cannot stray,
  I can never, never lose my way.

3 Let me love Thee more and more,
  Till this fleeting, fleeting life is o'er;
  Till my soul is lost in love,
  In a brighter, brighter world above.
                        Fanny J. Crosby.

Familiar Hymns.

292. MARTYN. 7s.

1 Jesus, Lover of my soul,
   Let me to Thy bosom fly,
  While the billows near me roll,
   While the tempest still is high:
  Hide me, O my Saviour! hide,
   Till the storm of life is past,
  Safe into the haven guide;
   Oh, receive my soul at last!

2 Other refuge have I none,
   Hangs my helpless soul on Thee;
  Leave, ah! leave me not alone,
   Still support and comfort me;
  All my trust on Thee is stayed,
   All my help from Thee I bring;
  Cover my defenceless head
   With the shadow of Thy wing.

3 Thou, O Christ, art all I want:
   More than all in Thee I find;
  Raise the fallen, cheer the faint,
   Heal the sick, and lead the blind;
  Just and holy is Thy name,
   I am all unrighteousness;
  Vile and full of sin I am,
   Thou art full of truth and grace.
                            C. Wesley.

293. BOYLSTON. S. M.

1 Blest be the tie that binds
   Our hearts in Christian love—
  The fellowship of kindred minds
   Is like to that above.

2 Before our Father's throne
   We pour our ardent prayers;
  Our fears, our hopes, our aims are one,
   Our comforts and our cares.

3 We share our mutual woes,
   Our mutual burdens bear,
  And often for each other flows
   The sympathizing tear.

4 The glorious hope revives
   Our courage by the way,
  While each in expectation lives,
   And longs to see the day.
                            J. Fawcett.

294. JEWETT. 6s.

1 My Jesus, as Thou wilt!
   Oh, may Thy will be mine!
  Into Thy hand of love
   I would my all resign:
  Through sorrow, or through joy,
   Conduct me as Thine own,
  And help me still to say,
   My Lord, Thy will be done!

2 My Jesus, as Thou wilt!
   Though seen through many a tear,
  Let not my star of hope
   Grow dim or disappear;
  Since Thou on earth hast wept
   And sorrowed oft alone,
  If I must weep with Thee,
   My Lord, Thy will be done!

3 My Jesus, as Thou wilt!
   All shall be well for me:
  Each changing future scene,
   I gladly trust with Thee;
  Then to my home above
   I travel calmly on,
  And sing, in life or death,
   My Lord, Thy will be done!
                            Tr. by J. Borthwick.

295. FOUNTAIN. C. M.

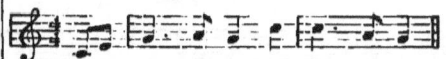

1 There is a fountain filled with blood,
   Drawn from Immanuel's veins;
  And sinners, plunged beneath that flood,
   Lose all their guilty stains.

2 Dear dying Lamb! Thy precious blood
   Shall never lose its power,
  Till all the ransomed church of God
   Be saved, to sin no more.

3 E'er since, by faith, I saw the stream
   Thy flowing wounds supply,
  Redeeming love has been my theme,
   And shall be till I die.

4 Then, in a nobler, sweeter song,
   I'll sing Thy power to save,
  When this poor lisping, stammering tongue
   Lies silent in the grave.

Familiar Hymns

296. ST. THOMAS. S. M.

1 I love Thy kingdom, Lord!
  The house of Thine abode,
The church, our blest Redeemer saved
  With His own precious blood.

2 I love Thy church, O God!
  Her walls before Thee stand,
Dear as the apple of Thine eye,
  And graven on Thy hand.

3 For her my tears shall fall,
  For her my prayers ascend;
To her my cares and toils be given,
  Till toils and cares shall end.
                    Timothy Dwight.

297. Tune—ITALIAN HYMN. Page 177

1 Come, Thou almighty King,
  Help us Thy name to sing,
    Help us to praise:
  Father! all-glorious,
  O'er all victorious,
  Come, and reign over us,
    Ancient of Days!

2 Come, Thou incarnate Word,
  Gird on Thy mighty sword;
    Our prayer attend;
  Come, and Thy people bless,
  And give Thy word success;
  Spirit of holiness!
    On us descend.

3 Come, holy Comforter!
  Thy sacred witness bear,
    In this glad hour:
  Thou, who almighty art,
  Now rule in every heart,
  And ne'er from us depart,
    Spirit of power!
                    C. Wesley.

298. Tune—ALETTA. Page 3.

1 They who seek the throne of grace
  Find that throne in every place,
  If we live a life of prayer,
  God is present everywhere.

2 In our sickness and our health,
  In our want, or in our wealth,
  If we look to God in prayer,
  God is present everywhere.

3 When our earthly comforts fail,
  When the woes of life prevail,
  'Tis the time for earnest prayer;
  God is present everywhere.

4 Then, my soul, in every strait,
  To thy Father come, and wait;
  He will answer every prayer:
  God is present everywhere.
                    Oliver Holden, alt.

299. BEAUTIFUL RIVER.

1 Shall we gather at the river,
  Where bright angel feet have trod—
  With its crystal tide forever
  Flowing from the throne of God?

Cho.—Yes, we'll gather at the river,
  The beautiful, the beautiful river—
  Gather with the saints at the river,
  That flows by the throne of God.

2 On the margin of the river,
  Washing up its silver spray,
  We will walk and worship ever
  All the happy, golden day.

3 Soon we'll reach the shining river,
  Soon our pilgrimage will cease:
  Soon our happy hearts will quiver
  With the melody of peace.
                    R. Lowry.

300. Tune—WORK. 7. 6.

1 Work! for the night is coming,
  Work thro' the morning hours;
  Work while the dew is sparkling,
  Work 'mid springing flowers;
  Work when the day grows brighter,
  Work in the glowing sun;
  Work, for the night is coming,
  When man's work is done.

2 Work! for the night is coming,
  Work in the sunny noon;
  Fill brightest hours with labor,
  Rest comes sure and soon.
  Give every flying minute
  Something to keep in store;
  Work, for the night is coming,
  When man works no more.
                    Annie L. Coghill.

Familiar Hymns.

301. MORE LOVE TO THEE.

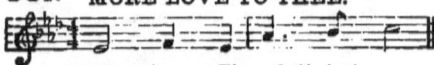

1 More love to Thee, O Christ!
   More love to Thee;
Hear thou the prayer I make
   On bended knee;
This is my earnest plea:
   More love, O Christ! to Thee,
   ||: More love to Thee. :||

2 Once earthly joy I craved,
   Sought peace and rest:
Now Thee alone I seek,
   Give what is best;
This all my prayer shall be,
   More love, O Christ! to Thee,
   ||: More love to Thee. :||

3 Then shall my latest breath
   Whisper Thy praise;
This be the parting cry,
   My heart shall raise,
This still its prayer shall be:
   More love, O Christ, to Thee,
   ||: More love to Thee. :||
Elizabeth Prentiss.

302.   TUNE—AMERICA. Page 177.

1 My country! 'tis of thee,
   Sweet land of liberty,
      Of thee I sing:
Land where my fathers died!
Land of the Pilgrims' pride!
From every mountain side
      Let freedom ring.

2 My native country, thee—
Land of the noble free—
      Thy name I love;
I love thy rocks and rills,
Thy woods and templed hills;
My heart with rapture thrills
      Like that above.

3 Let music swell the breeze,
And ring from all the trees
      Sweet freedom's song;
Let mortal tongues awake;
Let all that breathe partake;
Let rocks their silence break,—
      The sound prolong.

4 Our fathers' God! to Thee,
Author of Liberty,
      To Thee we sing:
Long may our land be bright
With freedom's holy light;
Protect us by Thy might,
      Great God, our King!
S. F. Smith.

303.   THE SOLID ROCK. L. M.

1 My hope is built on nothing less
Than Jesus' blood and righteousness;
I dare not trust the sweetest frame,
But wholly lean on Jesus' name:
On Christ, the solid rock, I stand;
All other ground is sinking sand.

2 When darkness seems to veil His face,
I rest on His unchanging grace;
In every high and stormy gale,
My anchor holds within the vail:
On Christ, the solid rock, I stand;
All other ground is sinking sand.
Edward Mote.

304.   HORTON. 7.

1 Come, said Jesus' sacred voice,
Come, and make my paths your choice;
I will guide you to your home,
Weary pilgrim, hither come!

2 Hither come! for here is found
Balm that flows for every wound,
Peace that ever shall endure,
Rest eternal, sacred, sure.
Ann L. Barbauld.

305.   TUNE—BETHANY. 6. 4.

1 Nearer, my God, to Thee,
   Nearer to Thee!
E'en though it be a cross
   That raiseth me,
Still all my song shall be,
||: Nearer, my God, to Thee, :||
   Nearer to Thee.

2 There let the way appear
   Steps up to heaven,—
All that Thou sendest me
   In mercy given,—
Angels to beckon me
||: Nearer, my God, to Thee, :||
   Nearer to Thee.

3 Then, with my waking thoughts
   Bright with Thy praise,
Out of my stony griefs
   Bethel I'll raise;
So by my woes to be
||: Nearer, my God, to Thee, :||
   Nearer to Thee.
Sarah F. Adams.

Familiar Hymns.

306. IOWA. S. M.

1 A charge to keep I have,
  A God to glorify,
  A never-dying soul to save,
  And fit it for the sky.

2 To serve the present age,
  My calling to fulfill;
  Oh, may it all my powers engage
  To do my Master's will.

3 Arm me with jealous care,
  As in Thy sight to live;
  And oh, Thy servant, Lord, prepare
  A strict account to give.

4 Help me to watch and pray,
  And on Thyself rely,
  Assured, if I my trust betray,
  I shall for ever die.
                                C. Wesley.

307. LYTE. 6. 4.

1 Jesus, Thy name I love,
  All other names above,
    Jesus, my Lord!
  Oh, Thou art all to me!
  Nothing to please I see,
  Nothing apart from Thee,
    Jesus, my Lord!

2 Thou, blessed Son of God,
  Hast bought me with Thy blood,
    Jesus, my Lord!
  Oh, how great is Thy love,
  All other loves above,
  Love that I daily prove,
    Jesus, my Lord!

3 When unto Thee I flee,
  Thou wilt my refuge be,
    Jesus, my Lord!
  What need I now to fear?
  What earthly grief or care,
  Since Thou art ever near?
    Jesus, my Lord!
                                J. G. Deck.

308. HURSLEY. L. M.

1 Sun of my soul, Thou Saviour dear,
  It is not night if Thou be near;
  Oh, may no earth-born cloud arise
  To hide Thee from Thy servant's eyes.

2 When the soft dews of kindly sleep
  My wearied eyelids gently steep,
  Be my last thought how sweet to rest
  Forever on my Saviour's breast.

3 Abide with me from morn till eve,
  For without Thee I cannot live;
  Abide with me when night is nigh,
  For without Thee I dare not die.
                                J. Keble.

309. THE PRECIOUS NAME.

1 Take the name of Jesus with you,
    Child of sorrow and of woe—
  It will joy and comfort give you,
    Take it, then, where'er you go.

CHO.—Precious name, O how sweet!
    Hope of earth and joy of heav'n,
  Precious name, O how sweet!
    Hope of earth and joy of heav'n.

2 O the precious name of Jesus!
    How it thrills our souls with joy,
  When His loving arms receive us,
    And His songs our tongues employ!

3 At the name of Jesus bowing,
    Falling prostrate at His feet,
  King of kings in heaven we'll crown Him,
    When our journey is complete.
                                Lydia Baxter.

310. THE ROCK THAT IS HIGHER.

1 Oh, sometimes the shadows are deep,
    And rough seems the path to the goal,
  And sorrows sometimes how they sweep,
    Like tempests down over the soul.

CHO.—Oh, then, to the Rock let me fly,
    To the Rock that is higher than I.

2 Oh, sometimes how long seems the day,
    And sometimes how weary my feet;
  But toiling in life's dusty way,
    The Rock's blessed shadow how sweet.

CHO.—Oh, then, to the Rock let me fly,
    To the Rock that is higher than I.

3 Oh, near to the Rock let me keep,
    If blessings, or sorrows prevail;
  Or climbing the mountain way steep,
    Or walking the shadowy vale.

CHO.—Then, quick to the Rock I can fly,
    To the Rock that is higher than I.
                                E. Johnson.

Familiar Hymns.

311. WHITER THAN SNOW.

1 Dear Jesus, I long to be perfectly whole,
   I want Thee forever to live in my soul;
   Break down every idol, cast out every foe—
   Now wash me, and I shall be whiter than
      snow.

Cho.—Whiter than snow, yes, whiter than snow:
   Now wash me, and I shall be whiter
      than snow.

2 Dear Jesus, come down from Thy throne in
      the skies,
   And help me to make a complete sacrifice;
   I give up myself, and whatever I know—
   Now wash me, and I shall be whiter than
      snow.
                              James Nicholson.

312. ST. GERTRUDE. 11.

1 Onward, Christian soldiers, marching as to
      war,
   With the cross of Jesus going on before;
   Christ the royal Master leads against the foe;
   Forward into battle, see His banners go.

2 Like a mighty army moves the Church of God;
   Brothers, we are treading where the saints
      have trod;
   We are not divided, all one body we,
   One in hope and doctrine, one in charity.

3 Crowns and thrones may perish, kingdoms
      rise and wane,
   But the Church of Jesus constant will remain;
   Gates of hell can never 'gainst that Church
      prevail;   [not fail.
   We have Christ's own promise, and that can-
                              S. Baring-Gould.

313. Tune—HENLEY. Page 120.

1 Come unto Me, when shadows darkly gather,
   When the sad heart is weary and distrest,
   Seeking for comfort from your heavenly Fa-
      ther,
   Come unto Me, and I will give you rest.

2 Large are the mansions in thy Father's dwell-
      ing,
   Glad are the homes that sorrows never dim,
   Sweet are the harps in holy music swelling,
   Soft are the tones which raise the heavenly
      hymn.

3 There, like an Eden blossoming in gladness,
   Bloom the fair flowers the earth too rudely
      pressed;
   Come unto me all ye who droop in sadness,
   Come unto me, and I will give you rest.
                              Catherine H Esling.

314. THE VALLEY OF BLESSING.

1 I have entered the valley of blessing so sweet,
   And Jesus abides with me there;
   And His spirit and blood make my cleansing
      complete,
   And His perfect love casteth out fear.

Cho.—Oh, come to the valley of blessing so
      sweet,
   Where Jesus will fullness bestow—
   And believe,and receive,and confess Him,
   That all His salvation may know.

2 There is peace in the valley of blessing so
      sweet,
   And plenty the land doth impart,
   And there's rest for the weary-worn traveler's
      feet,
   And joy for the sorrowing heart.
                              Annie Wittenmyer.

315. LUX BENIGNA. P. M.

1 Lead, kindly Light, amid th'encircling gloom,
      Lead Thou me on;
   The night is dark, and I am far from home;
      Lead Thou me on:
   Keep Thou my feet; I do not ask to see
   The distant scene; one step enough for me.

2 I was not ever thus, nor prayed that Thou
      Shouldst lead me on;
   I loved to choose and see my path; but now
      Lead Thou me on!
   I loved the garish day; and, spite of fears,
   Pride ruled my will: remember not past years.

3 So long Thy power has blest me, sure it still
      Will lead me on
   O'er moor and fen, o'er crag and torrent, till
      The night is gone,
   And with the morn those angel faces smile,
   Which I have loved long since, and lost a-
      while.   John Henry Newman.

4 Meanwhile along the narrow rugged path
      Thyself hath trod
   Lead, Saviour, lead me still in childlike faith
      Home to my God;
   To rest forever after earthly strife
   In the calm light of everlasting life.
                              E. H. Bickersteth.

Familiar Hymns

316. TRUSTING JESUS.

1 Simply trusting every day,
　Trusting through a stormy way;
　Even when my faith is small,
　Trusting Jesus, that is all.

Cho.—Trusting as the moments fly,
　　Trusting as the days go by;
　　Trusting Him, whate'er befall,
　　Trusting Jesus, that is all.

2 Brightly doth His Spirit shine
　Into this poor heart of mine;
　While He leads I cannot fall,
　Trusting Jesus, that is all.
　　　　　　　Edgar Page Stites.

317. Tune—ORIOLA. Page 8.

1 Dear Saviour, ever at my side,
　How loving Thou must be,
　To leave Thy home in heaven to guard
　A little child like me!
　Thy beautiful and shining face
　I see not, though so near;
　The sweetness of Thy soft, low voice
　I am too deaf to hear.

2 I cannot feel Thee touch my hand
　With pressure light and mild,
　To check me, as my mother did
　When I was but a child;
　But I have felt Thee in my thoughts
　Fighting with sin for me;
　And when my heart loves God, I know
　The sweetness is from Thee.
　　　　　　　F. W. Faber.

318. WOODWORTH. L. M.

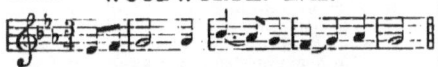

1 Just as I am, and waiting not
　To rid my soul of one dark blot:
　To Thee, whose blood can cleanse each spot,
　O Lamb of God! I come, I come!

2 Just as I am, though tossed about,
　With many a conflict, many a doubt,
　Fightings and fears, within—without:
　O Lamb of God! I come, I come!

3 Just as I am, Thou wilt receive,
　Wilt welcome, pardon, cleanse, relieve
　Because Thy promise I believe:
　O Lamb of God! I come, I come!

4 Just as I am, Thy love unknown
　Has broken every barrier down:
　Now to be Thine, yea, *Thine alone*,
　O Lamb of God! I come, I come!
　　　　　　　Charlotte Elliott.

319. DRAW ME NEARER.

1 I am Thine, O Lord, I have heard Thy voice,
　And it told Thy love to me;
　But I long to rise in the arms of faith,
　And be closer drawn to Thee.

Ref.—Draw me nearer, nearer blessed Lord,
　　To the cross where Thou hast died,
　　Draw me nearer, nearer blessed Lord,
　　To Thy precious, bleeding side.

2 Consecrate me now to Thy service, Lord,
　By the pow'r of grace divine;
　Let my soul look up with a steadfast hope,
　And my will be lost in Thine.

3 There are depths of love that I cannot know
　Till I cross the narrow sea,
　There are heights of joy that I may not reach
　Till I rest in peace with Thee.
　　　　　　　Fanny J. Crosby.

320. ABIDE WITH ME.

1 Abide with me! fast falls the eventide,
　The darkness deepens—Lord, with me abide!
　When other helpers fail, and comforts flee,
　Help of the helpless, oh, abide with me.

2 Swift to its close ebbs out life's little day;
　Earth's joys grow dim, its glories pass away;
　Change and decay in all around I see;
　O Thou who changest not, abide with me!

3 I need Thy presence every passing hour:
　What but Thy grace can foil the tempter's power.
　Who like Thyself my guide and stay can be?
　Through cloud and sunshine, Lord, abide with me.

4 I fear no foe, with Thee at hand to bless;
　Ills have no weight, and tears no bitterness:
　Where is death's sting? where, grave, Thy victory?
　I triumph still, if Thou abide with me.
　　　　　　　Henry Francis Lyte.

Familiar Hymns

321. HIDING IN THEE.

1 O safe to the Rock that is higher than I,
My soul in its conflicts and sorrows would fly;
So sinful, so weary, Thine, Thine would I be;
Thou blest "Rock of Ages," I'm hiding in Thee.

Ref.—Hiding in Thee, Hiding in Thee,
　Thou blest "Rock of Ages," I'm hiding in Thee.

2 In the calm of the noontide, in sorrow's lone hour,
In times when temptation casts o'er me its [power;
In the tempests of life, on its wide, heaving sea,
Thou blest "Rock of Ages," I'm hiding in Thee.

3 How oft in the conflict, when pressed by the foe,
I have fled to my Refuge and breathed out my woe;
How often when trials like sea-billows roll,
Have I hidden in Thee, O Thou Rock of my soul.
William O. Cushing.

322. AUTUMN. 8.7.

1 Glorious things of thee are spoken,
　Zion, city of our God!
He, whose word cannot be broken,
　Formed thee for His own abode:
On the Rock of Ages founded,
　What can shake thy sure repose?
With salvation's walls surrounded,
　Thou may'st smile at all thy foes.

2 See! the streams of living waters,
　Springing from eternal love,
Well supply thy sons and daughters,
　And all fear of want remove:
Who can faint, while such a river
　Ever flows their thirst to assuage?—
Grace, which, like the Lord, the Giver,
　Never fails from age to age.
J. Newton.

323. DENNIS. S. M.

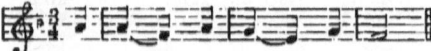

1 How gentle God's commands!
　How kind His precepts are!
Come, cast your burdens on the Lord,
　And trust His constant care.

2 His bounty will provide,
　His saints securely dwell;
That hand which bears creation up,
　Shall guard His children well.

3 Why should this anxious load
　Press down your weary mind?
Haste to your heavenly Father's throne,
　And sweet refreshment find.

4 His goodness stands approved,
　Unchanged from day to day;
I'll drop my burden at His feet,
　And bear a song away.
P. Doddridge.

324. Tune—RIALTO. S. M. Page 115.

1 Come, we who love the Lord,
　And let our joys be known;
Join in a song of sweet accord,
　And thus surround the throne.

2 Let those refuse to sing
　Who never knew our God;
But children of the heavenly King
　May speak their joys abroad.

3 The men of grace have found
　Glory begun below;
Celestial fruits on earthly ground
　From faith and hope may grow.

4 The hill of Zion yields
　A thousand sacred sweets,
Before we reach the heavenly fields,
　Or walk the golden streets.
Isaac Watts.

325. LEAD ME ON.

1 Traveling to the better land,
O'er the desert's scorching sand,
Father! let me grasp Thy hand;
　Lead me on, lead me on!

2 When at Marah, parched with heat,
I the sparkling fountain greet,
Make the bitter water sweet;
　Lead me on, lead me on!

3 Bid me stand on Nebo's height,
Gaze upon the land of light,
Then, transported with the sight,
　Lead me on, lead me on!

4 When I stand on Jordan's brink,
Never let me fear or shrink;
Hold me, Father, lest I sink:
　Lead me on, lead me on!

5 When the victory is won,
And eternal life begun,
Up to glory lead me on!
　Lead me on, lead me on!
Anon.

Familiar Hymns.

326. CORONATION. C. M.

1 All hail the power of Jesus' name!
   Let angels prostrate fall;
   Bring forth the royal diadem,
   And crown Him Lord of all.

2 Let high-born seraphs tune the lyre,
   And, as they tune it, fall
   Before His face who tunes their choir,
   And crown Him Lord of all.

3 Ye seed of Israel's chosen race,
   Ye ransomed of the fall,
   Hail Him who saves you by His grace,
   And crown Him Lord of all.

4 Hail Him, ye heirs of David's line,
   Whom David Lord did call:
   The God Incarnate, Man Divine;
   And crown Him Lord of all.

5 Sinners! whose love can ne'er forget
   The wormwood and the gall,
   Go, spread your trophies at His feet
   And crown Him Lord of all.

6 Let every tribe and every tongue,
   That bound Creation's call,
   Now shout, in universal song,
   The crownèd Lord of all.
                              Edward Perronet.

327. KÜCKEN. 7.

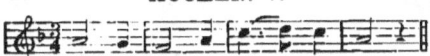

1 Quiet, Lord, my froward heart;
   Make me teachable and mild,
   Upright, simple, free from art;
   Make me as a weanèd child,—
   From distrust and envy free,
   Pleased with all that pleases Thee.

2 What Thou shalt to-day provide,
   Let me as a child receive;
   What to-morrow may betide,
   Calmly to Thy wisdom leave:
   'Tis enough that Thou wilt care;
   Why should I the burden bear?

3 As a little child relies
   On a care beyond his own,
   Knows he's neither strong nor wise,
   Fears to stir a step alone;
   Let me thus with Thee abide,
   As my Father, Guard, and Guide.
                              J. Newton.

328. HE LEADETH ME. L. M.

1 He leadeth me! oh, blessed thought,
   Oh, words with heavenly comfort fraught,
   Whate'er I do, where'er I be,
   Still 'tis God's hand that leadeth me!

Cho.—He leadeth me! He leadeth me!
   By His own hand He leadeth me;
   His faithful follower I would be,
   For by His hand He leadeth me.

2 Sometimes 'mid scenes of deepest gloom,
   Sometimes where Eden's bowers bloom,
   By waters still, o'er troubled sea—
   Still 'tis His hand that leadeth me.

3 Lord, I would clasp Thy hand in mine,
   Nor ever murmur nor repine—
   Content, whatever lot I see,
   Since 'tis my God that leadeth me.
                              Jos. H. Gilmore.

329. ANTIOCH. C. M.

1 Joy to the world—the Lord has come;
   Let earth receive her King;
   Let every heart prepare Him room,
   And heaven and nature sing.

2 Joy to the earth, the Saviour reigns;
   Let men their songs employ,
   While fields and floods, rocks, hills and plains
   Repeat the sounding joy.

3 He rules the world with truth and grace,
   And makes the nations prove
   The glories of His righteousness,
   And wonders of His love.
                              Isaac Watts.

330. HOLLEY. 7.

1 Softly now the light of day,
   Fades upon my sight away:
   Free from care, from labor free,
   Lord, I would commune with Thee.

2 Soon for me the light of day
   Shall for ever pass away;
   Then from sin and sorrow free,
   Take me Lord, to dwell with Thee.
                              Geo. Washington Doane.

Index of Subjects.

The Figures Refer to the Numbers.

ABIDE WITH ME, 44, 127, 172, 214, 320.
ABIDING IN CHRIST, 114, 122, 157, 158, 161, 291, 305, 314.
ACCESS TO GOD, 22, 157, 305, 318.
ADORATION OF CHRIST, 19, 20, 28, 50, 58, 61, 65, 68-73, 237, 238, 326.
ADVENT OF CHRIST,
    at birth, 46-51, 54-56, 329.
    to judgment, 252.
    to kingdom, 59, 142.
AFFLICTIONS, 24, 45, 125, 139, 187, 253-256, 276, 294, 313, 315.
ANGELS,
    at Advent of Christ, 26, 48-51, 53, 55.
    at Resurrection of Christ, 66, 67.
    Ministry of, 103, 253.
    Songs of, 26, 41, 50, 84.
ASPIRATION FOR GOD, 108, 159, 161, 305.
    for Christ, 127, 162, 301, 307, 319.
    for Heaven, 24, 88, 128, 262, 284.
    for Holiness, 111, 176, 311.
ASSURANCE, 146, 232.
ATONEMENT, 59, 70, 111, 118, 124, 134, 138, 174, 281, 285, 295, 318.

BEAUTIFUL CITY, 263.
    Land, 260, 269.
    River, 299.
BENEDICTION, 11, 13, 16.
BENEVOLENCE (see CHURCH and MISSIONS).
BETHLEHEM, 47-49.
BIBLE, 52, 77-83.
BREAD OF HEAVEN (see CHRIST).
BREAD OF LIFE (see CHRIST and BIBLE).
BREAKERS AHEAD, 194.
BREATH OF GOD, 176.
BRIDEGROOM, 252.
BROTHERLY LOVE (see CHRISTIAN FELLOWSHIP and COMMUNION OF SAINTS).

CHARITY, 133-137.
CHILDREN,
    Christian, 141, 317.
CHILDREN'S CROWNS, 271.
    Duty, 245.
    Praise, 28, 37, 55, 72.
    Prayer, 208, 209, 317.
CHILDHOOD OF JESUS, 48, 117, 209.
CHRIST ABIDING, 44, 172, 214, 320.
    Adoration of, 19, 20, 28, 50, 58, 61, 65, 68-73, 238, 326.
    Advent, first, 46-51, 54-56, 329.
        second, 59, 142, 252.
    Ascension, 67.
    at the door, 98.
    Atonement of, 59, 70, 111, 134, 138, 285, 295, 318.
    Blood of, 59, 70, 109, 111, 118, 124, 174, 285, 295, 318.
    Bread of Life, 20.
    Brother, 123, 127.
    Burden bearer, 104, 113, 123, 173.
    Burial of (see SEPULCHRE).
    Calling, 84-92, 96, 102, 110, 111, 118, 286, 304, 313.
    Captain, 184-186, 189, 191 (see SOLDIER).
    Child, 51, 55, 117, 209.
    Conqueror, 65.
    Coronation of, 326, 329.
    Cross of, 89, 109, 118, 138, 204, 233.
    Crucified, 30, 59, 134, 318.
    Day spring, 26.
    Divine, 19, 202, 281 (see TRINITY).
    (our) Endeavor, 190.
    Fountain, 124, 295.
    Friend, 32, 104, 127.
    Giver of all, 58.
    Guide, 68, 127, 132, 140, 149, 154, 178, 281.
    Hiding-place, 121, 140, 155.
    Holy, 201, 208, 209.
    Holy Child, 48.
    Incarnation, 46-51, 89, 95, 303.

    Indwelling, 172.
    Intercession of, 123, 254.
    Jesus, 69.
    Joy of, 20, 138.
    Judge, 105, 252.
    King, 10, 47, 50, 67, 185, 231, 239, 274, 329.
    Lamb of God, 281, 295, 318.
    Leader, 189, 193, 234, 325, 328.
    Life of men, 20.
    Life on earth, 57-61, 117, 127, 209.
    Light, 20, 48, 71, 73, 79, 138, 205, 264, 308, 315.
    Lord, 19, 48, 53, 120, 185.
    Love of, 30, 95, 104, 116, 117, 128, 138, 143, 273, 275, 280, 282, 292, 317.
    Master, 120, 179-181.
    Merciful, 101, 108.
    Morning Star, 73.
    Name of, 54, 69, 73, 120, 130, 151, 216, 309.
    Near, 120, 126, 319.
    Physician, 107.
    Pilot, 153, 194, 235, 276, 287.
    Precious, 124.
    Prince of Peace, 54, 222.
    Redeemer, 30, 34, 59, 70, 93, 134, 138, 174, 295 (see SAVIOUR).
    Refuge, 115, 139, 150, 191, 292.
    Reign of, 179, 231.
    Resurrection, 65-67.
    Rock, 30, 121, 150, 162, 285, 303, 310, 321.
    Saviour, 109, 210, 232, 281 (see REDEEMER).
    Seeking the lost, 53, 89, 90.
    Sepulchre, 62, 63, 66, 106.
    Shepherd, 30, 157, 166, 189.
    Son of God, 202.
    Star, 26, 68, 73, 192.
    Stilling the tempest, 61, 161, 175, 276, 287.
    Strong to save, 242.

Index of Subjects.—Continued.

Sufferings of, 30, 59, 193, 196, 204, 205.
Sun, 308.
Sympathy of, 93, 120, 123, 126, 131, 144.
Triumph of, 63–65, 67, 326, 329.
Trustworthy, 316 (see FAITH and TRUST).
Water of Life, 99.
Word, 297.
CHRISTIAN COMFORT, 91, 146, 182, 232, 238, 239, 281 (see TRUST).
Conflict, 196, 228, 254, 289 (see SOLDIER).
Courage, 151, 163, 184–196, 222, 237, 274, 312.
Duty, 53, 133, 180–183, 245, 300, 306.
Endeavor, 179–193.
Fellowship, 151, 179, 212, 219, 256, 270, 293.
Joy, 60, 123, 283, 324, 329.
Love to Christ, 19, 20, 62, 69, 70, 126–132, 162, 207, 291 (see ASPIRATION).
  to the Saints, 296 (see CHURCH and COMMUNION OF SAINTS).
Peace, 146, 161, 165, 175, 275.
Resignation, 45, 294, 327.
Safety, 92, 104, 143–158.
Trust, 43, 61, 140–168, 177, 211, 235, 276, 281, 291, 294, 316, 321, 323, 327, 328.
Union with Christ, 114, 122, 157, 158, 291, 305, 314.
CHRISTMAS HYMNS, 46–56.
CHURCH, 227, 229, 288, 321.
Beloved of God, 225, 322.
Beloved of Saints, 223, 296, 324 (see COMMUNION OF SAINTS).
Safety of, 145, 157, 322.
Triumph of, 222, 225, 226, 231, 236, 237, 242, 312, 321, 329.
Unity of, 24, 179, 212.
Work of, 53, 180–183, 190, 224, 272, 300 (see MISSIONS).
CITY OF GOD, 227.
CLOSE OF SERVICE, 3, 8, 11, 13–16, 277–279.
COMFORT (see AFFLICTION and CHRIST, and CHRISTIAN).
COMFORTER, THE, 74–76.
COMING TO CHRIST, 91, 177, 178, 318.
COMMANDMENTS, RESPONSE AFTER, 7.
COMMUNION OF SAINTS,
  With Christ, 53, 59, 95, 151.

  With each other, 164, 256, 257, 270, 293, 296.
CONFESSION, 85–87, 93, 109, 173, 272.
CONFLICT (see SOLDIER).
CONSECRATION, 108, 112, 124–129, 140, 169–178, 274, 283, 311, 316, 319.
CONVERSION, 111, 112, 129, 169, 172–174, 238, 273, 283, 285, 318.
COURAGE, 151, 163, 222 (see CHRISTIAN).
CROSS, 89, 109, 130, 138, 204, 233 (see CHRIST).
CROSSING THE BAR, 153.

DAY (see MORNING and EVENING).
DEATH, 153, 154.
DISMISSION (see CLOSE OF SERVICE).
DOUBT, 277–279.
DUTY, 53, 133, 180–183, 245, 300, 306.

EASTER, 63–66.
ENCOURAGEMENT, 182 (see CHRISTIAN and INVITATION).
ENDEAVOR, CHRISTIAN, 179–193.
ETERNITY, 252.
EVENING, 11–13, 164, 255, 308, 315.
  Prayer, 8, 14, 15, 167, 218, 320, 330.

FAITH, 113–125, 139–168, 281, 291, 294 (see TRUST and CHRISTIAN).
FATHER, HEAVENLY, 40–42.
FELLOWSHIP (see CHRISTIAN).
FORGIVENESS, 85, 86, 93, 108–111, 283.
FREE GRACE, 18, 101, 234.

GALILEE, 57, 120.
GLORIA PATRI, 5, 6.
GLORIA TIBI, 4, 189.
GOD, 25, 39–42, 58, 147, 250.
  Goodness of, 323.
  Law of, 275.
  Love of, 40, 42, 43, 158, 168, 170, 187, 239, 275.
  Wonderful works of, 31.
GOLDEN DAY, 179.
GOLDEN GATE OF PRAYER, 197.
GOOD SHEPHERD, 30, 157, 166, 189.
GOSPEL, 80, 81.
GRACE BEFORE MEALS, 1, 2.
GRATITUDE, 2, 15, 21, 23, 27, 31, 43, 117, 251 (see PRAISE).
GREAT PHYSICIAN, 107.
GROWTH IN GRACE, 108.
GUIDANCE, DIVINE, 156 (see CHRIST'S GUIDE).

HAPPINESS (see CHRISTIAN JOY).
HARVEST,
  Spiritual, 180, 181, 183, 248, 272.
  Temporal, 247, 248.
HEAVEN, 88, 100, 119, 125, 248, 255–271, 284, 299, 313.
  Christ in, 70, 265.
  Friends in, 256, 257, 260, 264, 265, 270.
  Home in, 119, 149, 260–267, 313.
  Rest in, 24, 34, 125, 259, 268, 269, 275, 313.
  Sought, 24, 88, 128.
HIDING PLACE, 121, 140, 155.
HOLY SPIRIT, 3, 74–76, 176, 177, 215.
HOMELAND, 119.
HOSANNA, 28, 72.

INVITATIONS OF THE GOSPEL, 84–104, 110 (see CHRIST CALLING).

JERUSALEM THE GOLDEN, 284.
JESUS (see CHRIST).
JOY, 60, 123, 283, 324, 329.
JUDGMENT, 25, 105, 252.
JUST FOR TO-DAY, 211.

KIND WORDS, 135.
KINDNESS, 133–137.
KING OF GLORY, 10, 47, 67.
KNOCKING, 98.
KYRIE ELEISON, 7.

LAMB OF GOD, 281, 295, 318.
LEANING ON JESUS, 154 (see CHRISTIAN COMFORT and TRUST).
LIFE,
  Brevity of, 39, 252, 258, 261.
  Divine, 127.
  Tree of, 230.
LIFE-LINE, 221.
LIGHT OF THE WORLD, 71, 73, 79.
LITANIES, 105, 201–210.
LONGING (see ASPIRATION).
LOOKING TO JESUS, 115.
LORD OF THE HARVEST, 248.
LORD'S DAY, 10, 18, 34–38 (see WORSHIP).
LORD'S SUPPER, 259.
LOVE OF GOD (see CHRIST and GOD).
  to God (See CHRISTIAN).
  Man, 133, 135–139.
  Saints (see COMMUNION OF SAINTS).

219

Index of Subjects.—Concluded.

MERCY,
  Freedom of, 101, 108, 234.
  Prayer for, 105, 216.
MERCY SEAT, 219.
MILLENNIUM, 222.
MISSIONARY'S CALL, 224.
MISSIONS, 221-230, 288, 290.

NATIONAL, 302.
NATURE, 21, 27, 248.
NEARNESS TO GOD, 305 (see CHRISTIAN).
NEW YEAR, 249, 250.
NOTHING BUT LEAVES, 272.

OLD, OLD STORY, 12, 42, 117, 280, 282.
OPENING OF SERVICE, 9, 10, 34-36.

PARDON (see FORGIVENESS).
PEACE, 146, 161, 165, 175, 275.
PENITENCE, 86, 87, 105-112, 272.
PRAISE, 4-6, 9, 18, 21-32, 42, 50, 188, 251.
  to Christ, 19, 20, 28, 30, 50, 58, 65, 232, 237, 240, 248, 326 (see ADORATION).
  to the Lord of the Harvest, 248.
  to the Trinity, 5, 6, 9, 18.
PRAISES, CHILDREN'S, 28, 55, 72.
PRAYER, 7, 131, 132, 152, 172, 197-220, 234, 298.
  and Watchfulness, 186, 195, 228, 252.
  Call to, 33, 186, 252.
  Children's, 208, 209, 317.
  Evening, 8, 10, 12, 14, 15.
  for Guidance, 132, 178.
  Pardon, 105, 107, 173 (see REPENTANCE).
  to the Father, 39, 40, 217, 218.
  to Christ, 19, 20, 43, 107, 109, 130, 173, 177, 201-209, 214, 281, 292, 301, 308, 317-320.
  to the Holy Spirit, 3, 74-76, 176, 215.
  to the Trinity, 167, 168, 170, 297.

PROMISES, 148 (see TRUST).
PROVIDENCES (see TRUST).

REDEMPTION, 30, 34, 59, 70, 93, 295.
RESCUE, 221.
RESIGNATION (see SUBMISSION).
RESPONSIBILITY, PERSONAL, 183.
REST IN GOD, 116, 147, 187, 232.
  of Heaven, 24, 34, 125, 259, 268, 269, 275, 313.
RESURRECTION, 64-67.
RIVER OF GOD, 81.
ROCK OF AGES, 39, 121, 150, 285, 303, 310, 321.
ROLLING ONWARD, 240.

SABBATH, 10, 18, 34-38 (see WORSHIP).
SABBATH BELLS, 35-38.
SAINTS (see CHURCH and COMMUNION OF SAINTS).
SENTENCES, 4-7.
SERVICES, OPENING AND CLOSING OF, 4-12.
SIN,
  Burden of, 93, 96, 98, 111, 173.
  Conflict with, 196, 228, 289 (see CHRISTIAN).
  Forgiveness of, 85, 86, 93, 108-111, 283.
  Sorrow for, 86, 87, 108, 109, 111, 272.
SINNERS (see INVITATION).
SOLDIER, CHRISTIAN, 151, 181, 184-186, 191, 193, 196, 228, 237, 241, 244, 246, 254, 274, 289, 312.
SORROW (see AFFLICTION and SIN).
SOWERS, 183 (see HARVEST).
STAR OF BETHLEHEM, 192.
SUBMISSION, 45, 294, 327.
SUNSHINE, 60.
SYMPATHY,
  Christian, 179, 212, 219, 270, 293, 296.
  of Christ, 93, 120, 123, 126, 131, 144.

TEMPERANCE, 184, 241-247.
TEMPTATION, 194-196, 221, 228, 254, 276, 289.
THANKSGIVING (see GRATITUDE).
TIMES AND SEASONS, 248-252.
TREE OF LIFE, 230.
TRINITY, 5, 6, 9, 18, 167, 168, 170, 297.
TRIUMPH, 25, 231-240 (see CHRIST and CHURCH).
TRUST, 43, 61, 140-168, 177, 211, 235, 276, 281, 294, 316, 321, 323.
  in Grace, 146, 150, 152, 154, 155, 158, 159, 161, 291.
  in Providence, 145, 147, 148, 156, 166, 327, 328.

UNDIQUE GLORIA, 29.
  Union with Christ, 114, 122, 157, 158, 291, 305, 314.
  with Saints, 151, 179, 212, 219, 256, 270, 293.

VOWS, 274.

WARFARE (see CHRISTIAN CONFLICT and SOLDIER).
WATCHFULNESS, 194, 196.
WATCHING AND PRAYING, 186, 195, 197, 228, 252.
WATER OF LIFE, 99.
WEARINESS, 87, 90, 96, 111, 113, 115, 116, 139, 196, 198, 310, 313.
WELL DONE, 255.
WELL WITH US, 143, 144, 146.
WOMAN'S CRUSADE, 241, 242.
WORD OF GOD (see BIBLE).
WORK, 53, 180, 181, 183, 190, 224, 272, 300.
WORSHIP, 5, 6, 9-32, 40, 41, 58, 160 (see PRAISE).

YEAR, NEW, 250, 251.
  Old, 252.

ZION, 288, 322 (see CHRIST).

GENERAL INDEX.

Titles in Small Caps—First Lines in Roman.

A.

	NO.
A BROTHER'S CARE	123
A charge to keep I have	306
A CROWN FOR THE YOUNG	271
A LITTLE TALK WITH JESUS	131
A TEMPERANCE SONG	246
Abide with me, fast falls the even-tide	320
ABIDING	114
Abiding, oh, so wondrous sweet	114
All hail the power of Jesus' name	326
ALL WILL BE WELL	143
Almighty God, when round their shrine	230
ANGEL VOICES EVER SINGING	41
ANOTHER YEAR IS DAWNING	249
ARISE AND SING	231
AS FLOWS THE RIVER	275
As helpless as a child who clings	159
Ask ye what great thing I know	134
As shadows cast by cloud and sun	192
As the distant streams uniting	240
AS TRUSTFUL AS A CHILD	159
At the golden gate of prayer	197

B.

BATTLE HYMN OF THE WOMEN'S CRUSADE	241
Be present at our table, Lord	2
BEAUTIFUL HILLS OF GLORY	266
BEAUTIFUL LAND OF REST	269
BENEATH HIS WING	158
Beyond the smiling and the weeping	261
BLESSED ASSURANCE	232
BLESSED HOME-LAND	262
BLESSED NIGHT	47
Blest be the tie that binds	293
BLEST DAY OF GOD! MOST BRIGHT	36
Blow winds of God, awake and blow	127
BOOK OF GRACE AND GLORY	77
BREAKERS AHEAD	194
Breaking thro' the clouds that gather	265
BREAK THOU THE BREAD OF LIFE	50
BREATHE ON ME, BREATH OF GOD	176
Bright and blessed morning	38
BRINGING IN THE SHEAVES	180
By Christ redeemed, in Christ restored	59
By faith I view my Saviour dying	101
By Thy birth, and by Thy tears	203

C.

	NO.
CARRY THE STANDARD BRAVELY	185
CAST THY BURDEN ON THE LORD	113
Child of God, when thou art weary	113
CHILDREN OF JERUSALEM	72
CHIME ON	37
CHRISTIAN! DOST THOU SEE THEM	196
Christian, seek not yet repose	228
CHRIST THE LORD COMES DOWN TO-NIGHT	53
CITY OF GOD	227
Come, children, now I pray	245
COME! COME TO JESUS!	97
COME, HEAVY-LADEN ONE	96
COME, HOLY GHOST, IN LOVE	76
COME HOME! COME HOME!	87
COME IN AND DWELL WITH ME	172
Come in, come in, O Saviour mine	172
COME, LET US ADORE HIM	23
COME, LET US ALL UNITE	170
Come, said Jesus' sacred voice	304
Come, Thou Almighty King	297
Come, Thou soul-transforming Spirit	3
COME TO JESUS! COME AWAY!	92
COME TO ME	91
Come unto Me, when shadows darkly	313
Come we who love the Lord	324
COME, YE FAITHFUL, RAISE THE STRAIN	64
Courage, brother, do not stumble	163
CROSSING THE BAR	153

D.

Dear Jesus, I long to be perfectly whole	311
DEAR LORD, REMEMBER ME	199
DEAR REFUGE OF MY WEARY SOUL	139
Dear Saviour, ever at my side	317
Dear Saviour, while on earth I stray	44
DO WHAT IS RIGHT	245

E.

Each cooing dove and sighing bough	57
Early, with blush of dawn	66
ERE I SLEEP	15
EVENING PRAYER	14

General Index.

F.

	NO.
Farewell, dear friends, adieu, adieu	13
Father of all from land and sea	212
Father, I know that all my life	156
FATHER OF MERCIES	40
Father, Thou art great and holy	178
Fear not, O little flock, the foe	145
Fierce raged the tempest o'er the deep	175
FLEE AS A BIRD	86
For all the saints, who from their labors	151
FOR CHRIST IS OUR ENDEAVOR	190
FOREVER BLESSED	151
Forsake me not! O Thou, my Lord	152
For the beauty of the earth	21
FROM EVERY STORMY WIND	219
From Greenland's icy mountains	290
From the hills and from the valleys	242
FROM THE RECESSES	217

G.

GIVE THANKS	31
Gliding o'er life's fitful waters	262
GLORIA	188
GLORIA PATRI	5–6
GLORIA TIBI	4
Glorious things of Thee are spoken	322
Glory be to the Father	5, 6
Glory, glory, glory be to Thee	4–188
GO AND TELL JESUS	93
GOD BE WITH YOU	16
God bless the noble band	243
GOD IS LOVE	42
God of pity, God of grace	207
God's free mercy streameth	234
God's mighty works, who can express?	31
God loved the world of sinners lost	273
GOD SPEED THE RIGHT	182
GOD WILL TAKE CARE OF YOU	147
GOLDEN GATE OF PRAYER	197
GOLDEN HARPS ARE SOUNDING	67
GOOD CHRISTIAN MEN, REJOICE	46
GOOD NIGHT	13
GRACE BEFORE MEALS	1
GUIDE US TO THEE	178

H.

HAIL THE CROSS OF JESUS!	233
HARK! HARK! MY SOUL	84
Hark! the sound of Angel voices	26
HARK! WHAT MEAN THOSE HOLY VOICES	50
HAVEN, BRIGHT HAVEN	267
HEAL ME, O MY SAVIOUR, HEAL	107
Hear the temperance call	214
He leadeth me! oh blessed thought	328
Heavenly Father, let Thy light	210
HIDE THOU ME	121
Holy Father, cheer our way	167
Holy Ghost, Comforter	74
Holy Ghost, the Infinite	215
HOME OF THE SOUL	260
HOSANNA WE SING	28
How gentle God's commands	323
How sweet is the Bible! how pure is the	52
HOW SWEET THE NAME OF JESUS SOUNDS	60

I.

I am safe in the Rock that is higher than I	150
I am Thine, O Lord, I have heard Thy voice	319
I AM TOILING ON A RESTLESS OCEAN	268
I BRING MY SINS TO THEE	173
I CANNOT ALWAYS TRACE THE WAY	43
I come, I rest beneath	158
I have entered the valley of blessing	314
I have read of a beautiful city	263
I heard the voice of Jesus say	286
I know not the way I am going	149
I know there's a crown for the saints	271
I KNOW THERE'S A REST	259
I LEFT IT ALL WITH JESUS	122
I LOVE TO HEAR THE STORY	117
I love to tell the story	282
I love Thy kingdom, Lord	296
I may not stay	142
I NEED THEE, PRECIOUS JESUS	124
I WANT TO BE AN ANGEL	88
I will sing you a song of that beautiful	260
IF I COULD ONLY KNOW	144
IN HEAVENLY LOVE ABIDING	157
In some way or other the Lord will provide	148
In the harvest-field there is work to do	181
IN THE HOUR OF TRIAL	254
IN THE SILENT MIDNIGHT WATCHES	98
In Thy cleft, O Rock of Ages	121
IT IS WELL WITH MY SOUL	146

J.

Jerusalem forever bright	269
Jerusalem the golden	284
JESUS CHRIST THE CRUCIFIED	134
Jesus, David's Root and Stem	309
JESUS, FROM THY THRONE ON HIGH	208
JESUS, HEED ME, LOST AND DYING	109
Jesus, in Thy dying woes	201
JESUS IS CALLING	90
Jesus is our Pilot	235
JESUS, KING OF GLORY	10
Jesus, Lover of my soul	292
JESUS, MY LORD, MY GOD, MY ALL	19
Jesus, my Saviour, to Bethlehem came	89
JESUS, OUR LIFE	20
Jesus, Saviour! hear my call	214
Jesus, Saviour, pilot me	287
JESUS, SON OF GOD MOST HIGH	202
Jesus, Thou joy of loving hearts	20
Jesus, Thy name I love	307
JESUS, WHO FOR US DIDST BEAR	204
Joy to the world—the Lord is come	329
Just as I am, and waiting not	318

K.

KEEP THOU MY WAY, O LORD	132
KIND WORDS CAN NEVER DIE	135
KYRIE ELEISON	7

L.

LABOR ON	181
Lead, kindly Light, amid th' encircling	315
LEANING ON THEE	154
Let all the world in every corner sing	29
LET THE GOOD ANGELS COME IN	103
Let us gather up the sunbeams	136
LET US PRAISE HIM TO-DAY	18
LIGHT AT EVENING TIME	167
Light of lights, with morning, shine	205
LIGHT OF THE WORLD, WE HAIL THEE	71
LITANY	201
Lo, a loving friend is waiting	102

General Index.

	NO.
Lo, Jehovah, His salvation	25
LOOKING HOMEWARD	264
LORD, ABIDE WITH ME	214
LORD, DISMISS US	277-279
LORD, FOR TO-MORROW	211
Lord, have mercy upon us	7
LORD, IN THIS, THY MERCY'S DAY	105
Lord of mercy and of might	206
LORD, THY WORD ABIDETH	83
LORD, WHAT OFFERING SHALL WE BRING	137
LOVE, REST AND HOME	261
LOVING INVITATION	102

M.

MARCH ONWARD!	191
MASTER, THE TEMPEST IS RAGING	276
May the grace of Christ our Saviour	278
MAY WE BE ONE	212
MEMORIES OF GALILEE	57
MISSIONARY'S CALL (Chant)	224
More love to Thee, O Christ!	301
My country, 'tis of thee	302
My faith looks up to Thee	281
My Father is rich in houses and lands	239
My God, my Father, while I stray	45
My God, is any hour so sweet	213
MY GOD, I THANK THEE	27
MY GUIDE	149
My heart is fixed, immortal God	171
My hope is built on nothing less	303
My Jesus, as Thou wilt	294
MY JESUS, I LOVE THEE	129
My soul, be on thy guard	289
My soul is not at rest	224

N.

Nearer, my God, to Thee	305
NOT HALF HAS EVER BEEN TOLD	263
NOTHING BUT LEAVES!	272
Now, God, be with us, for the night is	218
Now to Heaven our prayer ascending	182

O.

O BLESSED LORD, I COME	238
O CHURCH OF CHRIST	223
O EYES THAT ARE WEARY	115
O GOD, THE ROCK OF AGES	39
O GOLDEN DAY	179
O HAD I WINGS LIKE A DOVE	24
O HAPPY CHRISTIAN CHILDREN	141
O happy day that fixed my choice	283
O HAVE YOU NOT HEARD	99
O JESUS! LEAD US ONWARD	189
O Jesus, Saviour, hear my call	238
O LITTLE TOWN OF BETHLEHEM	48
O LORD, MY HEART IS THINE	140
O Lord of Heaven, and earth and sea	58
O LOVE, THAT WILL NOT LET ME GO	138
O MORNING STAR!	73
O MOST MERCIFUL	8
O PRAISE YE THE FATHER	9
O safe to the Rock that is higher	321
O SPIRIT OF THE LIVING LORD	75
O sweet sabbath bells!	35
O THE BITTER SHAME AND SORROW	108
O the name, the name of Jesus	130
O Thou, from whom all goodness flows	199
O Thou, in all Thy might so far	160
OH, ENTER IN!	94
OH, HOW HE LOVES	104
OH, PRAISE THE LORD	32
Oh, sometimes the shadows are deep	310
Oh, where are kings and empires	229
O'er the gloomy hills of darkness	226
One there is above all others	104
ONLY ONE PRAYER TO-DAY	216
ON THE MOUNTAIN'S TOP	225
Onward, Christian soldiers, marching as	312
OUR FATHER'S WILL	253
OUR SONG OF PRAISE	21

P.

PEACE, BE STILL!	175
Peaceful and beautiful haven of rest	267
PEACE, PERFECT PEACE	165
PRAISE HIM	30
Praise, O praise the Lord of harvest	248
PRAISE THE LORD OF HARVEST	248
PRAISE THE ROCK OF OUR SALVATION	17
Praise to Thee, Thou great Creator!	18
PRAY, ALWAYS PRAY	33
PRAY, BRETHREN, PRAY!	252
Prayer is the soul's sincere desire	200
PRAYER! SWEET PRAYER	220
PRAYER THE SOUL'S DESIRE	200

Q.

Quiet, Lord, my froward heart	327

R.

RAISE THE SONG OF TRIUMPH	237
Rejoice, rejoice, the promised time	222
RESURRECTION SONG	66
RESTING FROM HIS WORK TO-DAY	62
RESTING IN GOD'S LOVE	187
RESTING IN THY LOVE	116
RING, O YE MERRY BELLS	56
Rock of Ages, cleft for me!	285
ROLLING ONWARD	240

S.

Saviour, breathe an evening blessing	14
SAVIOUR, HELP ME	203
Saviour more than life to me	291
SCATTER SEEDS OF KINDNESS	136
SEEKING FOR ME	89
SENTENCE	4-7
Shall we gather at the river	299
SHALL WE KNOW EACH OTHER THERE?	257
SHELTERED IN THEE	150
SHINE ON, O STAR	68
SHINE OUT, OH LIFE DIVINE	127
Silently the shades of evening	164
Simply trusting every day	316
Since thy Father's arm sustains thee	187
SING A NEW SONG	25
SING OF JESUS, SING FOREVER	70
Sinner, to the Saviour clinging	110
Softly and tenderly Jesus is calling	90
Softly now the light of day	330
SOFTLY THE NIGHT IS SLEEPING	49
SOUND THE HIGH PRAISES OF JESUS	65
Sowing in the morning, sowing seeds	180
SPIRIT OF LOVE DIVINE	74
Standing at the portal of the opening year	250

General Index.

Title	No.
Star of peace to wanderers dreary	78
Strait is the gate, my child	94
STRIVE, WAIT, AND PRAY	186
Strive! yet I do not promise	186
Sun of my soul, Thou Saviour dear	308
Sunset and Evening Star	153
Sunshine in the soul	60
SWEETLY DAWNS THE SABBATH MORNING	34
SWEET SABBATH BELLS	35

T.

Title	No.
TAKE MY HEART, DEAR JESUS	169
Take the name of Jesus with you	300
Tell me the old, old story	280
TELL ME, YE WINGĒD WINDS	125
Ten thousand sowers thro' the land	183
TENTING BY THE SHORE	256
THANKS TO GOD	251
The banner cross is waving high	184
THE BRIGHT FOREVER	265
THE CHILD OF A KING	239
THE DAWNING LIGHT	142
The earth has grown old with its	51
The Homeland! O the Homeland!	119
The Light of truth is breaking	241
THE LORD BE WITH US	11
THE LORD IS MY SHEPHERD	166
THE LORD WILL PROVIDE	148
The morning light is breaking	288
THE NAME OF JESUS	130
THE OPENING YEAR	250
THE PROMISED TIME	222
The radiant morn has passed away	264
THE RIVER OF GOD	61
THE SABBATH CHIME	38
THE SOWERS	183
THE STAR OF BETHLEHEM	192
THE STRIFE IS O'ER	63
THE TEMPERANCE CALL	244
THE TREE OF LIFE	230
The twilight falls, the night is near	12
THE VOICE OF THE CHRIST-CHILD	51
THERE CAME A LITTLE CHILD TO EARTH	55
THERE IS A BETTER WORLD	100
There is a fountain filled with blood	295
There's a gentle voice within	112
There's sunshine in my soul to-day	60
There is a river deep and broad	81
They hover round us, bright angels	103
They who seek the throne of grace	298
THINE FOREVER! GOD OF LOVE!	168
THINE, LORD, FOREVER	174
THOU ART MY HIDING PLACE, O LORD	155
Though your sins be as scarlet	85
Thro' the love of God our Saviour	143
THROW OUT THE LIFE-LINE	221
THY WAYS ARE BEAUTIFUL	61
THY WORD IS A LAMP	79
THY WORD IS LIKE A DEEP MINE	82
'TIS SWEET TO KNOW	126
To-day Thy mercy calls me	118
TO JESUS I WILL GO	112
TO US A CHILD OF HOPE	54
TOUCH NOT THE CUP	247
Traveling to the better land	329
Trembling, they now behold	66
TRIUMPHANT ZION	236
TRUE-HEARTED, WHOLE-HEARTED	274
TRUSTFULLY, COME I TO THEE	177
Trustfully, trustfully, come I to Thee	177
TRUST IN GOD AND DO THE RIGHT	163

U.

Title	No.
UNDIQUE GLORIA	29

W.

Title	No.
WATCH AND PRAY	195
Watch, for the time is short	195
WATCHING AND PRAYER	228
WE ALL MIGHT DO GOOD	133
WEARY OF EARTH	111
Weeping as they go their way	106
We leave the world of care	37
WE MAY NOT CLIMB THE HEAVENLY STEEPS	120
We've launched our barque on the ocean	194
We would see Jesus—for the shadows	162
WHAT IS LIFE?	258
When peace like a river attendeth	146
WHEN SHALL WE MEET AGAIN?	270
WHEN TWILIGHT GATHERS FAST	255
WHEN THE WEARY, SEEKING REST	198
When torn is the bosom with sorrow	220
WHEN WINDS ARE RAGING	161
When we hear the music ringing	257
WHERE ARE KINGS AND EMPIRES NOW?	229
While way-worn and weary	116
WHO GIVEST ALL	58
WHO IS ON THE LORD'S SIDE?	193
With silence only as their benediction	253
With tearful eyes I look around	91
With Thy gifts Thy grace bestow	1
WONDERFUL LOVE	128
WONDERFUL STORY OF LOVE	95
WONDROUS LOVE	275
WORSHIP THE LORD	22
Work, for the night is coming	300

Y.

Title	No.
Yes, for me, for me He careth	123
Ye temperance warriors brave	246

www.ingramcontent.com/pod-product-compliance
Lightning Source LLC
Chambersburg PA
CBHW021844230426
43669CB00008B/1069